Difference
&
Identity

Difference

& Identity

A Theological Anthropology

Ian A. McFarland

THE
PILGRIM
PRESS
Cleveland

for Ann

The Pilgrim Press, 700 Prospect Avenue E.,
Cleveland, Ohio 44115-1100, U.S.A.
pilgrimpress.com

Portions of the text first appeared in "Who Is My Neighbor: The Good Samaritan as a Resource for Theological Anthropology," *Modern Theology* 17, no. 1 (January 2001): 57–66; in "A Canonical Reading of Ephesians 5:21-33: Theological Gleanings," *Theology Today* 57, no. 3 (October 2000): 344–56; and in "Personhood and the Problem of the Other," *Scottish Journal of Theology* (forthcoming).

06 05 04 03 02 01   5 4 3 2 1

Library of Congress Cataloging-in-Publication Data
McFarland, Ian A. (Ian Alexander), 1963–
    Difference & Identity : a theological anthropology / Ian A. McFarland.
      p. cm.
    Includes bibliographical references and index.
    ISBN 0-8298-1445-0 (alk. paper)
    1. Man (Theology). I. Title: Difference and identity. II. Title

BT701.2 .M274 2001
233 – dc21

                                        2001036574

Contents

Preface

The distinctiveness of human beings within creation lies not in any intrinsic qualities or capacities that people share, but rather, in the differences that mark their lives under God. The argument to support this thesis depends on appreciating the status of human beings as persons. While that in itself may seem anything but a novel claim, it takes a somewhat surprising form when the application of the term "person" in the human sphere is governed by its use in the doctrine of the Trinity.

This trinitarian strategy has a certain historical plausibility, in that modern reflection on personhood arguably has its roots in the Christian confession of God as three "persons" in one essence. Quite apart from issues of genealogy, however, the logic of Christian faith itself suggests that where both God and human beings are described as persons, it is the Creator and not the creature who should provide the reference point for our use of the term. In short, the theological claim that human beings are persons must be both justified and explicated in terms of what it means to speak of persons in connection with God.

While the rationale for making the term "person" the focal point of theological anthropology will be developed only over the course of the following chapters, the anticipated benefits of so doing can be stated fairly concisely. Attempts to define human personhood independently of trinitarian considerations invariably try to identify some common factor or factors that make someone a person. Anthropologies constructed on this basis have a difficult time assigning any positive significance to human difference and, indeed, are conceptually predisposed to interpret difference negatively, as something that obscures or even degrades the common core of personhood. By contrast, because the divine persons are identified precisely by what the Father, Son, and Holy Spirit do *not* share in common, the doctrine of the Trinity puts difference at the heart of personhood. An anthropology constructed on trinitarian grounds thus holds out the promise of an inclusivity that is not purchased at the price of forcing the bewildering diversity of human beings to fit a procrustean bed of underlying sameness.

Whether the book realizes this promise is another question. Where difference is affirmed as a central value, the possibility of drawing firm conclusions regarding human being is called into question. At the same time, it hardly makes sense to mount an argument at all unless one is prepared to risk a few generalizations. In my attempt to honor both these considerations, compromises have been unavoidable, and the resulting product is far from a comprehensive Christian doctrine of human being. It is more a series of progressive theological meditations, and my hope is that together they raise some pertinent questions and suggest a way of addressing them that, if not always convincing, at least contributes constructively to theological conversation.

For what is of value in these pages, the reader should thank my colleagues in the School of Divinity and Religious Studies at the University of Aberdeen. Their friendship and support over the last three years have been a constant source of encouragement. Special thanks are due to Iain Torrance and Francis Watson, whose questions and corrections were invaluable in the process of revising the manuscript for publication. I am also most grateful to George Graham and the rest of the editorial crew at Pilgrim Press for seeing this project through to print and patiently enduring requests for last-minute corrections to the text. It goes without saying that whatever faults remain are my responsibility and not theirs.

My deepest gratitude remains for my wife, Ann, who undertook the unlikely move from Honolulu to Aberdeen with characteristic grace and has continued unflappable as we have together adjusted both to a new culture and to the strange and joyous new world of parenthood. This book is dedicated to her.

The Difficulty of Defining Personhood

This book is a study in theological anthropology, or Christian reflection on human being. Its central theme is that knowing what we are as human beings is less important than knowing who makes us what we are. It is not my contention that this thesis is original. On the contrary, I view it as nothing more than a rephrasing of the biblical claim that our lives are "hidden with Christ in God" (Col. 3:3).[1] Its upshot is that even though we are not able to define what it is to be human, our destiny is secure in the one who made and redeemed us. In the words of another New Testament writer, "We are God's children now; it does not yet appear what we shall be, but we know that when he appears we shall be like him, for we shall see him as he is" (1 John 3:2, RSV; cf. Col. 3:4).

Deeply rooted in the tradition though my theme may be, however, it is far from self-evident. Nevertheless, I place it at the beginning because I find myself unable to identify any other starting point for this topic that seems less open to question. Since what will count as appropriate evidence and effective argumentation depends largely on the assumptions with which one begins, there seems no better strategy than simply to make a beginning and trust that the product that emerges will prove compelling, or at least interesting, enough to justify the chosen point of departure.

For this reason, the argument that follows is less an attempt to prove my thesis than to explicate its meaning. By way of introduction, however, I can note that one reason I begin where I do is that I

---

1. Except where otherwise indicated, quotations from the Bible are from the New Revised Standard Version or are my translations.

believe that the many attempts to define what we are as human beings have proved to be dead ends. They are dead ends in one respect because (as I shall have occasion to note at a number of points in what follows) they invariably entail the exclusion of significant categories of individuals on rather arbitrary grounds. But they are also dead ends because they tend more or less explicitly to measure human being in terms of conformity to some norm or standard—an approach that necessarily treats the differences between people as irrelevant to their identities as human beings.

EQUALITY, DIFFERENCE, AND DISCRIMINATION

In a society that continues to be scarred both by open bigotry and by myriad more subtle forms of discrimination based on the differences between people, highlighting difference as constitutive of identity may seem a questionable move. In this context, I have no wish to deny that a major (if by no means fully realized) accomplishment of the last two hundred years has been to erode the prejudices that have seen in the differences between people a rationale for excluding some from full participation in the life of society at large. Following the principles laid out in the American Declaration of Independence, people subject to indignity the world over have appealed to the principle that "all men are created equal" to demand recognition as human beings possessed of the same dignity and worthy of the same regard as anyone else. Though it has been subject to a continuous process of reinterpretation since it was first written, this one phrase has become the functional credo of the worldwide movement for human rights.

The undoubted good that has been accomplished by appeal to this phrase makes it difficult to criticize. Yet, notwithstanding the near universal acceptance now commanded by the principle that all human beings are created equal, the claim of the Declaration that this equality is "self-evident" is open to question. It is certainly not corroborated by a dispassionate assessment of the natural endowments of individuals. If anything is self-evident, it is surely that human beings differ enormously from one another: speed, strength, endurance, courage, wisdom, intelligence, compassion, and any other quality one might name are distributed most unequally among people.

An obvious rejoinder to this point is that the equality of which the

Declaration speaks is meant prescriptively rather than descriptively. In other words, what is "self-evident" is not that all human beings have the same endowments, but that the differences in their endowments should not be a bar to equal treatment.[2] Yet this response begs the question of *why* human beings should be treated as equals apart from an appeal to some state of affairs (e.g., some shared characteristic or property) that warrants their equal treatment.

In any case, no consensus has emerged regarding the qualities or capacities to be used as a reference point for equal treatment. The enormous diversity among human beings renders more inclusive criteria frustratingly vague and more concrete measures intolerably exclusive. What makes a particular individual a (fully) human being with a claim to "equal" status therefore remains a matter of debate. Thomas Jefferson himself was inclined to deny the full humanity of Africans on what he held to be objective, scientific grounds, and the nation he helped to found initially withheld equal participation in the rights of government from poor white men, people of color, and women of every race and class. Indeed, it is an ominous characteristic of the modern idea of equality that its emergence in the Enlightenment period went hand in hand with theories of racial and sexual difference that justified the exclusion of non-European men and all women from the equal status granted white men of property.[3]

While few today would accept the reasons that Jefferson used to support his views on the humanity of Africans as either objective or scientific,[4] agreement on the basis for affirming human equality remains elusive. One strategy is to correlate an individual's claim to equal treatment (or at least to basic rights) with her or his status as a *person*. The rhetorical appeal of this approach is reflected in the colloquial distinction between being treated "like a person" instead of "like a number" (when dealing with a bureaucracy) or "like a piece of meat" (when in a doctor's office). But what exactly does it mean

---

2. This position is defended by, among others, Peter Singer in his *Animal Liberation*, 2nd ed. (London: Jonathan Cape, 1990), 5.

3. According to Elisabeth Schüssler Fiorenza, the modern rhetoric of equality "has produced considerable inequalities because its standard and *tertium comparationis* for being human has been—and still is—the elite propertied educated man" (*Rhetoric and Ethic: The Politics of Biblical Studies* [Minneapolis: Fortress, 1999], 158).

4. For a survey of scientific arguments impugning the full humanity of various groups, see Stephen J. Gould, *The Mismeasure of Man* (New York: W. W. Norton, 1981).

to be treated in this way? Why is it desirable to be a person? And on what basis do we claim that status?

A THEOLOGICAL APPROACH

Given the wealth of important material on the topic of personhood that has been produced by scholars working with the tools of critical theory, neuroscience, phenomenology, philosophy, psychology, sociology, as well as the many subdisciplines of anthropology, it is necessary to say something about the sources and methods I use in addressing these questions. This study is specifically theological. While I seek to remain in dialogue with other disciplines, I do not pretend to be conversant with any more than a small fraction of the material available from them. I draw on this material eclectically but also selectively, with the result that much of undoubted value is simply left out. Readers will find the influence of feminists, literary theorists, and philosophers more in evidence than that of natural and social scientists.[5]

These omissions in my use of nontheological resources do not mean that I find the work of scientists uninteresting or unimportant, but only that it does not bear as directly on the questions of interest to me as the work of scholars in other fields. My choice of dialogue partners therefore should not be interpreted as a judgment about the absolute value of any particular discipline. As philosophers of language have argued for some time now, phenomena are patient of more than one kind of explanation. Various types or levels of explanation need not directly contradict one another, but neither are they reducible to a single way of speaking. Instead, given forms of explanation are appropriate to particular circumstances and should be evaluated according to their own standards (so that, for instance, a physiologist's account of a ballet will be different from an art critic's). Because my central concern is who makes us what we are rather than what we are as such, the kinds of explanation that interest me (e.g., how we identify or describe a particular someone) have more in common with those of philosophy and critical theory than with the results of scientific re-

---

5. For theological studies of human being in closer dialogue with the natural sciences than my own, see Philip Hefner, *The Human Factor: Evolution, Culture, and Religion* (Minneapolis: Fortress, 1993), and Wolfhart Pannenberg, *Anthropology in Theological Perspective* (Edinburgh: Clark, 1985).

search—though I hope that scientists will not find what I have to say to be in obvious contradiction with (even if it is not directly supported by) their own research.

Even where I draw on sources from outside of theology, my way of using them is governed by theological concerns. In an earlier book, I argued that one of the most important of these was the need to test the authenticity of Christian proclamation against its reception as "good news" by those at the margins of the church.[6] My aim was to avoid the simple juxtaposition of biblical and experiential criteria (whether in the mode of a Tillichian system of correlation or the elevation of present experience over tradition characteristic of some liberation theologies) by arguing that the character of the biblical witness was not consistent with any systematic demarcation of these two spheres. Because Jesus' status as Savior is inseparable from his ongoing commitment to the life of the church, he cannot be identified apart from reference to its sociopolitical contours.

I concluded that while the claims of the marginalized cannot be understood as a norm of Christian theology set over against Christ, neither is it possible to view the Christian kerygma as a fixed datum without reference to the reception of that proclamation by those at the margins. In line with this concern, my use of sources in this study is not governed by any theological "method," in the sense of an ordered set of protocols for deriving orthodox doctrines. Instead, I follow a more ad hoc procedure of attempting to tease out the logic of the tradition in light of what I perceive as ongoing challenges to its claim to preach the good news of Jesus to the poor.

It is my sense that this way of proceeding helps to check both naked biblicism and ecclesiastical triumphalism. In order to distinguish the church's inevitably biased and in any case provisional understandings of who Jesus is and what his identity implies for Christian faith and practice, it helps to look beyond the boundaries of the church, not in an archeological "quest for the historical Jesus," but rather, by way of a critical encounter with the "little ones" with whom Jesus identified himself. If they do not recognize the church's proclamation as "good

---

6. Ian A. McFarland, *Listening to the Least: Doing Theology from the Outside In* (Cleveland: Pilgrim, 1998).

news," then the church has good reason to question whether the Savior it proclaims is truly Jesus of Nazareth.

With respect to issues of theological anthropology in particular, the problematic character of the reception of the gospel at the church's margins is fairly clear. Although there is broad theological consensus regarding the central place of Jesus as the touchstone for Christian talk about human being, large numbers of people find themselves unable to hear what the church has to say about being human as good news for them. For many women, in particular, Jesus has been presented as a model for human life in a way that renders those who do not share his gender less than fully human. Still more broadly, Christians of European descent have all too frequently understood their own identity as normative in a way that has led them to denigrate or even deny the humanity of those whose skin color and cultural practices differ from their own. Given this legacy, it is hardly surprising that critics both within and outside of the church have regarded the "news" that Jesus is the measure of genuine humanity as less than "good."

Over against these more dominant strands of Christian practice, however, there are also the repeated irruptions of those who have seen in the figure of Jesus grounds for challenging narrower interpretations of humanity promoted by Christians and non-Christians alike. Given the difficulty that these voices have had in being heard, the mere fact of their existence does not by itself address the concerns of those who question whether a Christian understanding of human being is genuinely good news. Nevertheless, these alternative positions do suggest that the Christian tradition possesses resources, however inadequately developed, for challenging those narrower visions of human being that have had so devastating an impact on the shape of contemporary Western society. The theological challenge lies in showing that an anthropology that incorporates these more disruptive features represents a plausible interpretation of Christian belief.

THE CATEGORY OF THE PERSON

Though it plays a central role in many anthropologies, it is open to question whether invoking the category of the person is theologically either an effective or appropriate means for affirming the full humanity of marginalized groups. However broadly or narrowly the term "person" may be defined, its deployment as part of a strategy for affirming human equality tends to suppress the differences between people. On one level this is precisely the point: to the extent that the fact of difference is used as a rationale for denying some people the rights of which the Declaration of Independence speaks, one way of promoting the dignity of all is to deny that such differences are relevant to an individual's status as a person. This strategy corresponds to a general trend in the modern period toward the homogenization of experience. In the same way that seventeenth-century thinkers began to insist that natural phenomena in general should be described in terms of a fixed set of discrete, measurable features without reference to their wider contexts, so it seemed desirable to define an individual's humanity without reference to the particularities of family, culture, or tradition.[7]

As noted above, however, the internal logic of this strategy invariably raises the question of what those properties are that qualify any given individual as a person. In mathematics, equal quantities may be substituted for one another, and the rhetoric of equality likewise implies some underlying commonality. If persons are equal because they are at some level the same, then nonpersons may be withheld such consideration because they lack this underlying sameness. There is no positive role for difference within such an anthropology: where it is judged to be real, it is a mark of inequality; where it is viewed as merely a matter of appearance, it needs to be eliminated, or at least studiously ignored.[8]

Needless to say, any number of possible answers can be given to the question of what constitutes the underlying sameness of human persons. As the curtain was falling on the ancient world, Boethius defined a person as "the individual substance of a rational nature,"[9] and this correlation of personhood with self-conscious rationality has proved

---

7. For a detailed discussion of how the homogenization of reality was seen as crucial to the understanding and control of nature and society in Enlightenment thought, see Amos Funkenstein, *Theology and the Scientific Imagination from the Middle Ages to the Seventeenth Century* (Princeton: Princeton University Press, 1986), esp. 68–72, 342–45.

8. See Schüssler Fiorenza, *Rhetoric and Ethic*, 158.

9. *"Naturae rationabilis individua substantia"* (A Treatise against Eutyches and Nestorius, in *The Theological Tractates* and *The Consolation of Philosophy*, Loeb Classical Library [Cambridge: Harvard University Press, 1973], 84–85).

8 of the person.[10]

Although various criteria are invoked in contemporary discussions of what makes someone a person, appeals to cognitive function (understood chiefly as a mark of the capacity for self-determination) continue to play an important role.[11] And while it is no longer fashionable for such criteria to be deployed in a way that suggests a correlation between personhood and race or gender,[12] continued focus on cognition means that newborn infants and the severely retarded may still fail to qualify.[13]

Nor are the disadvantages of a definition of human being in terms of some anthropological lowest common denominator limited to those whose divergence from the norm causes them to be excluded from consideration as persons. Even those who make the cut may find themselves marginalized by established views of what it means to be a person. Because the criteria used to define personhood are in practice shaped by the dominant group within society, acknowledgment as a person invariably brings with it pressure to assimilate to this norm. This tendency leads some feminists to worry that gains achieved in the battle against sexual discrimination often have less to do with the affirmation of women as women than with women acquiring the "right" to participate more fully in forms of domination developed by men.[14] Members of other traditionally marginalized groups raise simi-

---

10. See, for example, Locke's classical liberal definition of a person as "a thinking intelligent being, that has reason and reflection, and can consider itself as itself, the same thinking thing, in different times and places" ("Personal Identity," bk. 2, ch. 27, §9 of *An Essay Concerning Human Understanding*, ed. Peter H. Nidditch [New York: Oxford University Press, 1975], 335).

11. For example, intelligence remains the "cardinal indicator" among Joseph Fletcher's fifteen benchmarks of "humanhood." Joseph Fletcher, "Indicators of Humanhood," *Hastings Center Report* (November 1972): 1–3.

12. For an exception to this general rule, see Richard J. Herrnstein and Charles Murray, *The Bell Curve: Intelligence and Class Structure in American Life* (New York: Free Press, 1994). Stephen J. Gould offers a short but convincing refutation of Herrnstein and Murray's argument in the revised edition of *The Mismeasure of Man* (London: Penguin, 1997), 367–78.

13. See, for example, Michael Toole, "A Defense of Abortion and Infanticide," in *The Problem of Abortion*, ed. Joel Feinberg (Belmont, Calif.: Wadsworth, 1973), 51–91; cf. the more detailed argument in his monograph *Abortion and Infanticide* (New York: Oxford University Press, 1983).

14. For example, although Rosemary Radford Ruether objects to Mary Daly's contemptuous dismissal of socially and economically successful females as "hench-women," she acknowledges the problems posed for women by pressure to assimilate to the male norm (*Women and Redemption: A Theological History* [London: SCM, 1998], 220–21).

lar concerns regarding the ways in which the norm of the propertied white male underlying the Jeffersonian vision of equality serves to mask ongoing practices of oppression and exclusion.[15]

Granted that difference ought not automatically be viewed negatively as reason for impugning someone's personhood, the fact that the Enlightenment's correlation of equality with uniformity seems unable to provide a sufficiently inclusive understanding of human being at least raises the question of whether difference should not be interpreted positively as constitutive of personal identity. Unfortunately, it is not at all clear how *difference* can be employed as a criterion of the personal. After all, the act of predication by which we call someone a person involves subsuming a particular individual ("Mary") under a general category ("person"). This linguistic fact would seem to imply that the individual in question possesses certain characteristics making it more appropriate to describe her as a person than a chair. From this perspective, defining "person" in terms of difference would seem to render the term vacuous by making it impossible to invoke definite criteria for distinguishing between what is a person and what is not.

If, however, we reconceive our analysis of persons in terms of who makes us persons rather than by trying to define what a person is, then the situation changes. Once this switch is made, our status as persons, instead of being understood as a function of some *thing* supposed to inhere in our physical or psychological makeup, can be reconceived as the result of some *one* acting toward us in a particular way. The activity of this someone may be a factor that all persons share in common, but it remains external to the individual. As a result, it is possible that every person may be constituted *as* a person differently, since it is the relation to this someone, and not the individual qualities that may shape or be shaped by this relationship, that counts.

In this context, it is worth noting that the interests that determined Boethius's definition of a person were not anthropological but theological. His intention was to explain to his Latin audience how the

---

15. See, for example, James H. Cone's criticism of white integrationist views of racial equality, *God of the Oppressed* (San Francisco: Harper & Row, 1975), 45–53, and Elizabeth Stuart's remarks on liberal denunciations of homophobia, "Sex in Heaven: The Queering of Theological Discourse on Sexuality," in *Sex These Days: Essays on Theology, Sexuality and Society*, ed. Jon Davies and Gerard Loughlin (Sheffield: Sheffield Academic Press, 1997), 184–204.

word "person" was to be understood in the doctrine of the Trinity. That he had to do this highlights the fact that the concept of the person as a particular kind of entity—so fundamental to the sensibilities of modern Western culture—was not a basic category of classical thought.[16] It emerged only in the fourth century as Christians tried to explain what they meant by the seemingly incoherent assertion that the New Testament terms "Father," "Son," and "Holy Spirit" referred to entities that were both genuinely distinct from each other and yet still just one God. What emerged was the trinitarian claim that Father, Son, and Spirit were three "persons" in one essence. Because each person was understood to coinhere in the others, they were not three gods but one. Yet they remained distinct as persons by virtue of their differing relationships with each other—relationships that characterized the unique way in which each was the one God. In this context, the term "person" referred not to any quality that the three had in common, but precisely to their irreducible difference from one another.

A TRINITARIAN FRAMEWORK

In the chapters that follow, I use this trinitarian framework to provide an account of human personhood that gives a positive role to difference. I do this by arguing that our claim to be persons is derived from our relationship to the triune God. It is therefore not rooted in any property or collection of properties that we possess as individuals, but in the fact that we stand in a certain relationship to the divine persons. This relationship is not one in which we naturally exist, nor is it one we secure for ourselves; rather, our being in relationship with God depends on the prior fact that God has chosen to live in relationship with us (1 John 4:19).

This divine choice takes concrete form when God comes among us as one of us in Jesus of Nazareth. In this one respect, our claim to personhood is based on a shared characteristic: we all stand in relationship to this one man. But this characteristic is not a property that can be derived from an examination of the individual. The fact

16. See John D. Zizioulas, *Being as Communion: Studies in Personhood and the Church* (Crestwood, N.Y.: St. Vladimir's Seminary Press, 1985), 32; cf. 27–28.

of anyone's being a person cannot be determined by looking at her or him in isolation, but only by examining that person's relationship to Jesus. It is Jesus who, as one of the divine persons, establishes us as human persons.

Difference is integral to this account of personhood, since no two people stand in the same relationship to Jesus. My relationship to him is very different from that of Mary Magdalene or Pontius Pilate. It follows that no two of us are persons in the same way, just as no two of the trinitarian hypostases are persons in the same way. Even though it is true that we all stand equally in the shadow of Jesus' cross, none of us occupies the same place under that cross. Peter stands in a place different from that of Judas or John, even though in every case it is Jesus who provides the necessary reference point for determining one's place—and thus one's own specific identity as a person.

The succeeding chapters are an effort to work out the implications of this trinitarian framework, with its emphasis on the constitutive role of difference, for the practice of identifying both others and ourselves as persons. Chapter 2 takes the form of a rather general reflection on how our ways of talking about persons affect our assessment of others as persons. The insights of poststructuralist thinkers in particular are used to analyze the ways in which the language we use to talk about others blocks our acknowledgement of them as persons who are (for that reason) different from ourselves. I then offer some preliminary reflections on how the biblical depiction of Jesus provides a narrative framework capable of overcoming this blockage by directing us to the other as someone whose identity as a person may be understood in terms of difference from ourselves.

This preliminary study sets the tone for the rest of the book, in which the figure of Jesus serves as the central reference point for a series of progressively broader characterizations of the diversity of human personhood. Chapter 3 focuses specifically on Jesus' status as the source of human personhood by tracing the development of "person" as a technical theological term through the trinitarian and christological controversies of the fourth, fifth, and sixth centuries. Chapter 4 then explores how Jesus' personhood shapes our own through reflection on the biblical image of the body of Christ. Especially as developed in the later Pauline literature, the language of the body provides a means of expressing both our subordination to Christ as "head" and our difference from Christ and each other as persons whose status as "members" of the body is not reducible to any common essence.

The next three chapters deal with the interpersonal dimensions of the christological framework laid out in chapters 3 and 4. Chapter 5 argues that the christological matrix of our personhood rules out the possibility of direct encounter between any two human persons. Because (in line with the analysis presented in chapter 2) the categories in which we speak of persons invariably block our perception of the other as a person, we can encounter the other as a person only through Jesus: he defines the other as a person by directing us to her or him. This argument is supported and illustrated through an exegesis of the parable of the good Samaritan as the biblical episode in which Jesus addresses most directly the question of who counts as a person.

Given that Jesus is not physically present among us, but (according to orthodox Christian belief) has ascended to God's right hand, chapter 6 offers an account of how Jesus mediates our encounters with others by reference to his presence in the Spirit on the one hand, and in the church on the other. These two dimensions of Jesus' presence, while closely interrelated, are distinguished as complementary ways of understanding how he encounters us in the present. Talk of the Spirit highlights Jesus' freedom both from the constraints of time and space and from human control. By contrast, the reality of the church connects Jesus' presence with the concrete reality of other human beings. Together, these two closely interrelated modes of Jesus' presence suggest that our life as persons is realized through communion in Christ with those who are different from us.

This situation raises the question of how I should conceive my relationship with a neighbor whose irreducible difference both from myself and from every other person would appear to make recourse to generalized rules of ethical conduct problematic. This problem is explored in chapter 7, with reference to the case of gender difference. Proceeding by way of an extended exegesis of the last third of Ephesians 5, I conclude that taking difference seriously makes it advisable to conceive of the relationship between persons in terms of reciprocity rather than equality. To focus on reciprocity is to recognize that the relationships between persons are characterized by a definite order, but also allows that the order is subject to change and development in light of the evolving character of each person's unique calling.

Having stressed the importance of difference in defining our identity as persons, I turn in chapters 8 and 9 to the question of the common nature that marks us as specifically human (as opposed to divine) persons. Here, too, the Trinity serves as the starting point for reflection on the relationship between personal difference and shared nature. In God, the divine nature is not prior to the distinction of the persons of the Trinity; rather, the unity of the divine nature is defined by the relationships in which the persons stand to one another. Following this model, I argue that human nature should not be conceived primarily as an ontological precondition of personal existence, but as an eschatological reality defined by the emerging pattern of relationships between those summoned by God in Christ. At the same time, I contend that in light of this call it is possible to identify certain "symptoms" of the human that mark out the created ground (though not the cause or condition) of our lives as persons, without which our destiny could only be interpreted as a negation rather than the gracious fulfillment of our creaturely existence.

The theological anthropology that results from this study does not provide easy answers to the ethical dilemmas that surround the question of personhood. Focus on the one who makes us persons over what a person is does not render issues like abortion, euthanasia, or gender politics ethically transparent. But it does suggest that the central question that should govern my decision making when addressing these issues is not, "Is this other a person?" but rather, "How do I show myself to be a person to this other?" After all, if difference is integral to our being persons, then there is no set of criteria that I can infallibly apply to decide on the personhood of the other. The best I can do is to consider the one who claims me as a person and attempt to discern the form that that claim takes in a given situation. In the process, I do not so much discover *what* a person is as come to be reminded *how* a person is.

- 2 -

Persons and the
Problem of Difference

The question of what it means to be a person is hardly new in theology, but it has been posed with renewed urgency over the past generation. On the one hand, traditional answers have been challenged by those whose personhood had long been viewed inside and outside the church as somehow inferior or deficient (especially men of color, and women of all backgrounds). On the other hand, reflection on the situation of people suffering from severe mental retardation, psychosis, and dementia has cast doubt on ancient and modern attempts to understand personhood in terms of self-consciousness or some other mental capacity.

The word "person" derives from the Latin term for a social, legal, or theatrical role (a meaning preserved in the English transliteration "persona"). One's "person" was defined by the part one played, whether on the stage or in society at large.[1] Today, there is an instinctive urge to recoil from this conception of what it means to be a person. Being a person is understood to be something far more fundamental than any role we play. Although a person may have many roles—chemist, mother, wife, daughter, administrator—she is only one person; and while roles can change, personhood tends to be conceived as an inalienable part of who we are.[2]

---

1. Even though Cicero describes persons as characterized both by a shared rational nature and by individual particularity (*De officiis* 1.107), "there is always an echo of the theatrical background (that is, the 'role' the individual has to play in life)" (Hans Urs von Balthasar, *Dramatis Personae: Persons in Christ*, vol. 3 of *Theo-Drama: Theological Dramatic Theory*, trans. Graham Harrison [San Francisco: Ignatius, 1992], 210).

2. See John D. Zizioulas, *Being as Communion: Studies in Personhood and the Church* (Crestwood, N.Y.: St. Vladimir's Seminary Press, 1985), 33–35.

In light of the importance of relationships in giving shape to our lives, some have argued that our personhood is constituted by our relations with God and each other, as these are formed through a cumulative pattern of address and response.[3] The problem is that such a definition appears to leave out those who for whatever reason are not able to respond to God's address in any recognizable manner.[4] In light of this difficulty, it seems preferable to view personhood as the basis for our relationships with each other rather than their product. In short, it is because we are persons that we have the capacity for relationship, not the other way around.[5]

This perspective seems broadly consistent with the biblical account of creation, in which the distinctiveness of the human creature lies primarily in God's decision to relate to it in a particular way rather than in its inherent abilities. In Genesis 1, for example, human beings are distinguished as the product of the divine decision to make a creature to oversee the rest of creation as God's plenipotentiary (Gen. 1:26–27). Although humanity is said to have been created "in the image of God," the text nowhere equates the divine image with the possession of any specific ability. Similarly, the second creation narrative relates that God, having breathed life in to Adam (Gen. 2:7), gave him responsibility for keeping the garden (v. 15) and naming the other creatures (v. 19); but at no point are these privileges correlated with any particular capacity. Needless to say, this is not to deny that human beings have capacities—they could hardly "fill the earth and subdue it" without them—or that these capacities might include self-consciousness, rationality, will, openness to the transcendent, and the like. It is simply to argue that such capacities are better deduced

---

3. See, for example, Alistair I. McFadyen, *The Call to Personhood: A Christian Theory of the Individual in Social Relationships* (Cambridge: Cambridge University Press, 1990), esp. 69–78.

4. McFadyen wants to avoid any such exclusion, arguing that "mere personal presence is enough to make some sort of claim for recognition" on the part of those who cannot communicate; but it is not clear how this idea squares with his earlier claim that "there is essence and personal identity only in communication" (McFadyen, *Call to Personhood*, 180, 156).

5. See the critique of relational models of personhood in Harriet A. Harris, "Should We Say That Personhood Is Relational?" *Scottish Journal of Theology* 51, no. 2 (1998): 214–34. Cf. John Macmurray, *Persons in Relation* (Atlantic Highlands, N.J.: Humanities Press International, 1991), 48–51.

a posteriori from the life for which God has elected humankind than posited as prior conditions of this election.[6]

And yet, as shown by the debate between Las Casas and Sepúlveda over the personhood of native Americans,[7] the witness of the creation narratives does not eliminate the possibility of disagreement over who is a legitimate heir of the dignity that God grants to Adam. Detaching the status of "person" from the possession of particular capacities therefore does not by itself guarantee that the resulting understanding of personhood will include all persons. However self-evident someone's personhood may be to one observer, others may be expected to call it into question. Even where the respect due to human beings is located exclusively in their status as creatures of God, the need to specify how the respect owed human beings as persons differs from that owing to other creatures leaves room for disagreement over which beings are to be treated as persons.[8]

THE PROBLEM OF THE OTHER

The analysis of language offered by poststructuralists suggests that merely formulating more inclusive definitions of the word "person" cannot solve this perennial problem. Poststructuralist theory is grounded in Ferdinand de Saussure's insight that meaning is generated by phonetic and semantic oppositions between words.[9] This play of differences between words is closely intertwined with what is viewed as normative in particular communities of discourse. For example, to the extent that "man" is defined by opposition to "woman" and functions as the generic term for "person," the personhood of women is occluded. In this way (as feminist theorists have long noted), "woman"

6. See chapter 9 for further discussion of this point.

7. For analysis of the dynamics that shaped this debate, see Tzvetan Todorov, *The Conquest of America: The Question of the Other* (New York: Harper & Row, 1984), 146–67 and passim. Cf. Gustavo Gutiérrez, *Las Casas: In Search of the Poor of Jesus Christ* (Maryknoll, N.Y.: Orbis, 1993), esp. chs. 5 and 6.

8. While Kathryn Tanner asserts that human beings are owed respect solely by virtue of their status as God's creatures, her admission that "the minimum standards of well-being to which one has a right will obviously vary depending upon the creature at issue" implies that some other quality or qualities besides the fact of creaturehood contribute to our ethical perspective on fellow human beings (*The Politics of God: Christian Theologies and Social Justice* [Minneapolis: Fortress, 1992], 179).

9. See Ferdinand de Saussure, *Course in General Linguistics* (Chicago: Open Court, 1988).

serves as the foundation upon which patriarchal views of humanity rest.[10]

Because semantic differentiation is intrinsic to the generation of meaning in language, no system of discourse can be fully inclusive: some "other" is always left over—and thereby left out.[11] Broadening the relevant definition (e.g., by explicitly including "women" in the definition of "mankind") cannot resolve the problem, because it does not change the underlying system of differences. Such inclusion simply "incorporat[es] the Other under the terms of the current discursive regime."[12] As a result, the differences that mark the other are homogenized rather than affirmed.

Deconstructionists have exploited these insights to argue that the semantic foundation laid by the excluded other is inherently unstable, since the system of differences between words is not grounded in anything other than established patterns of use. Because the accumulated weight of linguistic practice is the only basis for semantic stability, the other that grounds meaning in a discursive system is also a potential source of destabilization, precisely by virtue of its role in anchoring the system as a whole. Once identified, the occluded other exposes the fact that no configuration is exempt from the threat of further destabilization, because there is no point at which the play of differences between words comes to an end.[13]

As Mary McClintock Fulkerson points out, however, a theology that incorporates these ideas is not necessarily driven to relativism, since the possibility of exposing the process of occlusion is logically independent of the commitments and aims that lead one to do so. One may have no interest beyond exposing the "play of differences" in language, but one might equally well be motivated by concern for the

---

10. See, for example, the essays by Paula M. Cooey, Janet R. Jakobsen, and Mary McClintock Fulkerson in *Horizons in Feminist Theology: Identity, Tradition, and Norms*, ed. Rebecca S. Chopp and Sheila Greeve Davaney (Minneapolis: Fortress, 1997).

11. According to Emmanuel Levinas, the goal of Western philosophy from Plato to Heidegger has been the overcoming (and thus the exclusion or denial) of the other. See, for instance, Emmanuel Levinas, "Ethics as First Philosophy," in *The Levinas Reader*, ed. Seán Hand (Oxford: Basil Blackwell, 1989), 77; cf. his *Totality and Infinity: An Essay on Exteriority* (Pittsburgh: Duquesne University Press, 1969), 33–40.

12. Mary McClintock Fulkerson, "Contesting the Gendered Subject: A Feminist Account of the *Imago Dei*," in Chopp and Davaney, eds., *Horizons in Feminist Theology*, 107.

13. See Charles Taylor, *Erring: A Postmodern A/theology* (Chicago: University of Chicago Press, 1984), 108–9.

promotion of social justice.[14] In this context, Fulkerson maintains that the impossibility of creating a fully inclusive system of discourse does not prevent the episodic performance of "good sentences" that identify who is excluded at any given time from established definitions of, for example, personhood.[15] The question for theologians, she maintains, is how these episodic events can be linked together in a self-critical program of Christian practice.

Fulkerson proposes that narrative provides a category that allows feminists in particular to maintain a given set of commitments (specifically, to the liberation of women) without succumbing to the kind of totalizing language that promotes the occlusion of the other. She defines narrative (in contrast to explanation) as that feature of storytelling that focuses on the "what for" of events. In distinction from diachronic accounts of how particular situations arose, narrative is a rhetorical mode that relates different situations synchronically within some larger story of the world.[16] Because the synchronic mode highlights contrasts between different situations, it is a more effective tool for calling particular developments into question than diachronic accounts. The trick lies in finding a narrative framework that resists complacency with respect to the reality of new "others" hidden even in discourse that has successfully unearthed past practices of occlusion.

Suspecting that the narratives of liberal humanism may be too limited to serve as such a story, Fulkerson proposes instead "an incomplete story of a God-loved creation" that allows "commitment to the particular situation to develop new sensibilities for the outside."[17] Because no story is free of an "outside," and because the boundaries that mark every such outside are inherently fluid, what is to be hoped for is not a single liberating story but a series of stories that are able to affirm the partial as partial. In this way, she hopes it will prove possible to develop practices that "enable us to...hear from rather than explain the Other."[18]

---

14. Elisabeth Schüssler Fiorenza makes the same point in *Rhetoric and Ethic: The Politics of Biblical Studies* (Minneapolis: Fortress, 1999), 42–46.
15. Fulkerson, "Contesting the Gendered Subject," 111.
16. Ibid., 112.
17. Ibid., 114.
18. Ibid., 115.

HUMAN BEINGS
IN THE GOSPEL NARRATIVES

Fulkerson's emphasis on narrative as a means of affirming political commitments without necessarily subscribing to totalizing constructions provides a framework for reclaiming the etymological connection between being a person and having a role. This approach need not imply that personhood can be taken on or off like a mask, so long as the role in question has an inalienable quality to it.[19] Nor does such an understanding equate personhood with the possession of a particular set of capacities. After all, a character in a novel does not cease to be a character with the onset of Alzheimer's disease; nor does the fact of severe mental retardation prevent someone from being a character.

The problem comes in defining the story in which one's personal role is established. If the story is defined too narrowly (i.e., in terms of career, or of a significant friendship), then any lack, deficiency, or alteration in the relation between character and the story line is sufficient to cast doubt on an individual's status as a person. Alternatively, defining the narrative more broadly entails a degree of generalization that occludes the particularity of individual roles. For these reasons, it seems a bad idea (as Fulkerson suggests) to try to encompass the diversity of claimants to personhood in a single, grand narrative.

Christians' commitment to reading the Bible as a single narrative (albeit one containing many distinct genres) would therefore appear to cast doubt on the possibility of using scripture as the basis for an account of personhood that avoids totalizing pretensions. Nevertheless, I suggest that a person is best described theologically as a certain kind of character in the biblical story. Specifically (insofar as there are other "characters" in this story whom we would probably not want to call persons, like the stars that fight against Sisera in Judg. 5:20), a person is the kind of character to whom God proclaims the good news in Jesus of Nazareth. Three things need to be said in connection with this proposal.

The first is that what is intended here is a description rather than a definition. It is not that any one character (or even any sum of characters) in the biblical narrative encapsulates some identifiable essence

---

19. Cf. von Balthasar, *Persons in Christ*, esp. ch. 2.B.

of personhood, but that the story of Jesus is the central reference point for Christian talk about persons. Personhood is not, in other words, reducible to a certain set of qualities that Jesus exemplifies; it is simply shorthand for the kind of character the biblical God is depicted as addressing in Jesus.

Second, God's proclamation of the good news in Jesus is not simply to be identified with Jesus' speaking as such. Jesus addresses many "characters" in the Gospels, including various unclean spirits, a fig tree, and the wind on the Sea of Galilee; but these instances of speech do not have as their content the good news that Jesus both proclaims and embodies. That news is quite specifically the advent of God's reign (though it need not always take the form "The kingdom of heaven is at hand"). In other words, in the Gospels personhood is not a correlative of divine speech in general, but of speech that takes the particular form of gospel.

It is tempting at this juncture to highlight the diversity of those to whom Jesus proclaims the gospel: Jews and Gentiles, men and women, Pharisees and Samaritans, lepers and scribes, even the dead alongside the living (Mark 5:41; Luke 7:14; John 11:43). As striking as this diversity is, however, it does not provide any firm criteria for describing the kind of character God addresses in Jesus. Apart from the ability to isolate some particular character as somehow exemplary of what a person is, the variety of Jesus' addressees risks either opening the door to an indefinite number of rival views of personhood or abstracting the personhood of the Gospel characters from their distinctive identities.

In this context, a third point to be made is that Jesus himself is one of those to whom the gospel is addressed. If Jesus, as the Word of God incarnate, is the *autobasilea* who represents the reign of God in himself, as a fully human being he is also one to whom the reign is proclaimed. In fact (as Christians have affirmed from the very beginning), he is the first to taste the life of God's reign (1 Cor. 15:20–23) and, in this sense, is the person par excellence.

THE OTHER AND THE STORY OF JESUS

One way of characterizing Jesus' central status in Christian talk about persons is to use the language of the *imago Dei*. If other human beings are created *in* the image of God (Gen. 1:26–27), for the writers of the New Testament, Jesus *is* God's image (2 Cor. 4:4; Col. 1:15; cf. Heb. 1:3).[20] Insofar as Jesus is a particular individual, however, he, too, can only be identified by reference to a series of oppositions that distinguish him from other characters in the biblical narrative. Most obviously, as a Jewish man, he is contrasted with Gentiles and women (see especially Matt. 15:22–27 and par.; John 4:16–22); but he is also contrasted with Jewish scribes (Matt. 7:29; Mark 1:22), John the Baptist (Matt. 3:11 and pars.), Abraham (John 8:58), Moses (John 1:17), and even his own family (Mark 3:21, 32–35 and pars.). Focus on Jesus therefore by no means eliminates the problem of the other. The Johannine opposition between Jesus and "the Jews" in particular is a reminder of the church's tragically consistent practice of excluding the children of Israel from consideration as the object of God's gracious address.

To be sure, there are also narrative counterindicators to this pattern of characterizing Jesus in terms of opposition to others. In addition to being distinguished over against various groups and individuals, Jesus is also identified by his commitment to sinners (Matt. 9:13 and pars.) and children (Matt. 19:14 and pars.), as well as to the more amorphous category of the "least of these" (Matt. 25:31–46; cf. Matt. 18:6 and pars.). Yet the very breadth of these categories raises the suspicion that others are included only at the price of obliterating their particularity. And given that even these more inclusive strands of the canonical depiction of Jesus invariably rest upon some excluded other, the hermeneutical privileging of these texts does not resolve the problems associated with Christian claims for Jesus' normative status.

I therefore suggest that focusing on the patterns of *difference* by which Jesus is identified in the New Testament represents the most promising strategy for defending the central role Christians attribute to him. These patterns are by no means exhausted by figures listed above. Indeed, insofar as the decisive way in which Jesus is identified in the Gospels is as the one who been raised from the dead, his status as the risen Savior entails difference *from himself* as the one who died on the

---

20. Though the link between the Pauline characterization of Jesus as the image of God and the creation narratives is disputed, Francis Watson points out that the correlation of the term "image" and the language of creation in both Col. 3:9–11 and 2 Cor. 4:6 supports the contention that these passages allude to Genesis 1 (*Text and Truth: Redefining Biblical Theology* [Edinburgh: Clark, 1997], 281–82). See pp. 31–32 below for further discussion of this issue.

cross. This is certainly not to say that he is a different individual than the crucified one, but rather, to emphasize that he can be identified as the same only by way of contrast with what appeared on Good Friday to be his final destiny. As risen, Jesus is *not* dead, with the paradoxical result that his identity as the one who *was* dead (and thus the whole of his earthly career as the ground of that identity) is the decisive category of otherness that founds the Christian identification of him as Lord (see Rev. 1:18; cf. 1:5; 2:8).

Though poststructuralist analysis suggests that the other over against which a term is (implicitly) defined within a given cultural-linguistic framework is necessarily occluded, the narrative depiction of Jesus in the Gospels seems to work against this process. Because the primary "other" in terms of which Jesus is confessed as risen Lord is none other than Jesus the crucified, the very process that would normally hide this other brings him into the open. In answer to the question of who the risen one is, the reader of the New Testament is pointed squarely to examine the one he is "not"—the dead Jesus who hangs on the cross. In this way, the form of this particular narrative subverts the occlusion of the other in terms of which the norm is defined.

Perhaps more importantly, this process of unearthing the other does not come to a halt with the crucified Jesus. The identification of the exalted Savior with the crucified carpenter injects a certain instability into the "image of God" that this man instantiates. If we want to know what this image is, the Gospel narratives point us to the risen one; but in the very process of pointing to him they direct us to the crucified man on Golgotha and, thereby, to the various other reputable and disreputable characters who he also is not, but with whom his narratively rendered identity is irrevocably linked. In short, the resurrection short-circuits the process whereby the distinctiveness of the other is occluded. In rising from the dead, Jesus explicitly directs us to the other, so that to look at Jesus becomes the means for perceiving the other as other.

This suggests that the *imago Dei* is properly conceived not as a model to which individual beings may or may not conform, but as a lens through which individuals can be perceived as persons. That human beings are created "in" this image thus means that they are the kind of being whose personhood is disclosed through Jesus. We are persons because Jesus claims us as such, not because we possess a certain set of intrinsic ontological properties.

This way of interpreting the *imago Dei* also provides a useful frame-work for interpreting the more anthropologically inclusive passages of the New Testament. For example, it suggests that the point of the claim that in Christ there is "no longer Jew nor Greek, there is no longer slave or free, there is no longer male and female" (Gal. 3:28) is not that the differences between persons are obliterated by Christ (as though the other ceased to be other), but that difference ceases to be an occasion for exclusion. The other who differs from Jesus becomes the one through whom Jesus shows us who he is. Because in baptism we have put on Christ (Gal. 3:27), our identities are a function of Jesus' identity, and thus bound up with the others who stand behind any given identification of Jesus.

It follows that if we want to encounter Jesus, it is the other whom we need to meet, because it is as we encounter the other that we encounter Jesus (Matt. 25:40, 45; cf. 18:5 and pars.). Herein lies a seeming paradox that shapes the logic of faith: Jesus is the one person through whom the personhood of others is visible, not only because others have their personhood through Jesus, but also because Jesus claims his distinctive personhood as Savior only through the other. Consequently, the affirmation of Jesus as *imago Dei* need not result in a totalitarian collapsing of every person into Jesus, but can result in a movement of release in which Jesus' own distinctive identity draws us to look to the other in relation to whom his own career and destiny assume their particular shape.[21]

AFFIRMING OTHERS AS PERSONS

The particularity of the Christian narrative thus allows humans to be characterized as persons without depending on a formal definition of personhood in terms of intrinsic properties or qualities. Our being persons is simply a function of our having been addressed by God in Jesus, quite apart from how we may respond to that address. In looking at Jesus, we see what it means to be a person; but the content of what we see is not yet fully determined, since Jesus' identity as the risen

---

21. See chapter 5 for further development of this point.

one directs us to the bewildering diversity of characters (including both the dead and the not yet born) from which his own particular identity as a person cannot be separated.

At this point, it needs to be asked whether or not the characterization of personhood laid out here avoids the problem of homogenization. While I have maintained that attention to the identity of Jesus allows the reader to affirm the other in her or his otherness, it might appear that this approach merely produces a "generic other" that is too amorphous to valorize the excluded in a way that presents a genuine challenge to established ways of conceiving personhood.

I have no way of answering this objection directly, for despite my own language in the foregoing pages, the fact is that texts—even the biblical texts—do not "subvert" ideas or "direct" actions; people do. What I have suggested is a way of construing the New Testament witness to Jesus in a way that provides a basis for acting in a certain way with respect to the use of the word "person." The reading I propose will not produce the results I suggest without a commitment on the part of readers to put it into practice, because the identity of the outsider in any particular case cannot be determined apart from the particular context within which the biblical story of Jesus is read.

Nevertheless, I think that there are ways of characterizing persons in the present that provide at least a preliminary check against the homogenization of the other. These ways do not proceed by explicitly including certain groups under the category of the *imago Dei*. Rather, they proceed by a process of denying that particular categories of person are the *imago*.

Mary Fulkerson advocates just such an approach in the essay to which I have already referred. In concluding her own reflections on the theological appropriation of the *imago Dei*, she writes the following:

> Poststructuralism reminds us that there must be a purely negative function for the claim that woman is created *imago*...
> [namely,] that "men are not" *imago Dei* because the need to affirm *women* is constructed out of a pernicious system of significations which constitute *men*. This is not to say that woman is the real image of God; it is not even to say that both are. It is only to say that in this particular set of discursive arrangements,

in this context of male dominance, what the reigning discursive system means by *man* is not the *imago Dei.*[22]

Fulkerson's move here brings into relief the fact that unearthing the other undercuts established ways of speaking. Only so can the other be affirmed *as* other, without being subsumed under existing categories in a way that smoothes away her or his particularity. So from a feminist perspective, it is fruitless merely to affirm that women are also created in the image of God. On the one hand, such an approach merely subsumes women under the generic man; on the other hand, it posits its own excluded "other" (as women of color have been quick to note).

What Fulkerson does not address explicitly is the basis on which she affirms that "men are not" *imago Dei.* Emphasis on Jesus' status as the image of God may prove able to provide good christological grounds for her conclusions. Jesus, as the true image of God, is identified in scripture as the risen one, and thus the one who is not in the tomb. Once again, the instability built into this way of describing Jesus suggests that it is not in the resurrected one considered in isolation that the *imago Dei* is found. This is not to deny that Jesus is risen from the dead, but only to suggest that in seeking the *imago,* we, like the disciples at the ascension, are told not to look toward heaven.

In other words, the reason we can say that "what the reigning discursive system means by *man* is not the *imago Dei*" is that in looking to Jesus we are called to look away from him. It is important to attend to this order: looking away from Jesus is not the first but the second step, and is justified only on the basis of what we see when we look to him. We are not justified in looking away from Jesus by some independent insight into the nature of personhood that renders attention to him unnecessary. Instead, we are compelled to do so by the fact that by leaving the tomb and ascending to the right hand of God, Jesus does not allow us to contemplate him as the image of God in isolation. Rather (and in line with the teaching on the last judgment in Matthew 25), his status as the *imago* lies in the fact that he asks us to count as persons those who are most emphatically *not* the same as he.

---

22. Fulkerson, "Contesting the Gendered Subject," 114.

This does not mean that we can encounter persons apart from Jesus; on the contrary, we are able to encounter others as persons only insofar as we have already encountered Jesus. The point is that encountering Jesus is not an end in itself. Jesus himself makes this clear in his great valedictory prayer of John 17, where his repeated petition to God is that his disciples "may be one, as we are one" (vv. 11, 22; cf. 21, 23). For in the context of a world filled with religions promising unity with the divine, the special claim of Christianity was not that it provided a means of being one with God, but its declaration that through the activity of God, human beings had been made one with each other (see Eph. 2:13–15).

It follows that one task of the church as it looks to Jesus is (only seemingly paradoxically) to identify as persons those who are least like Jesus. By looking to Jesus we are prevented from taking our cue from those whose personhood seems the most self-evident (because most like ourselves) and challenged instead to consider as persons those we are inclined to view as somehow unworthy or deficient.[23]

THE SCRIPTURAL UNDERDETERMINATION OF PERSONS

Because the peculiar identity of Jesus as the image of God presents an ongoing challenge to the norms that are invariably established in every attempt to talk about persons, theological anthropology is advised against attempting to draw closer to truth about human personhood by presenting ever more precise definitions of what a person is. Instead, its most important assertions may be expected to take the form of denials that a particular type of individual defines personhood. The anthropologies that result will be limited and fragmentary, but may for that very reason prove more flexible—and thus more useful—as the context of Christian proclamation changes.

From this perspective, the task of theological anthropology is less a matter of defining ontological categories than of guiding and correcting the church's preaching. As the first human being who experiences the good news of the kingdom, Jesus is the touchstone for Christian

---

23. David Ford speaks of Christ as "a self-effacing face, referring us to the Father and to the faces of human beings" (*Self and Salvation: Being Transformed* [Cambridge: Cambridge University Press, 1999], 214; cf. 129).

talk about human personhood. But when we look at this person in the fullness of his glory, we find ourselves asked by him to look to the other whom he might otherwise conceal but to whom his ministry is in fact oriented.

Consequently, Jesus' status as *imago Dei* does not mean that he exhausts the content of personhood, or even that he exemplifies certain "personal" qualities. As the one who is himself the content of the gospel, he is also the original in whose image all those to whom the gospel is addressed have been created. But the features of this original are such that when we seek to describe what he is like, we are not permitted to treat him as an ideal against whom others are to be measured and to whom they may be judged to conform more or less closely. Instead, we find that he places our efforts at such categorization under judgment.

In this respect, the personhood Jesus instantiates is radically underdetermined. What it permits (and indeed demands) is a rejection of every ideology that holds up a particular category of person (whether "men" or "whites" or some other group) as normative. For the kind of character whom God addresses in Jesus—and thus the kind of character Jesus is—stands behind any such category as the occluded ground of its perceived normativity.

It follows that the content of personhood does not lie on the surface of human language or of human experience. The personhood of others—and, no less importantly, of ourselves—does not consist in conformity to what we imagine persons to be. Rather, we are instructed to seek what it means to be a person—to be an object of God's promise of the kingdom—in what is alien to our sensibilities and prejudices. In this sense, what it means to be a person is yet to be revealed. To paraphrase 1 John 3:2, though we are addressed as persons now, we do not yet fully know in what our personhood consists, because Jesus has not yet entered into the full number of relationships that shape his own personal identity.

The content of personhood is thus something that we can approach only by a series of exclusions, as we are led by the Spirit of Jesus to name those who precisely by virtue of their implicit claims to normative status do *not* point us to the *imago Dei* in the world. Because new norms displace old ones, and a shift in social location can radically alter the discursive landscape, the results we achieve will never be more than provisional. Yet this fact is no cause for despondency, because the Christian story does not presume that we know what it means to be a person. What it means to be a person is something that we can only anticipate in the encounter with those who, insofar as they are not like Jesus, remind us who Jesus is.

This approach has the advantage of avoiding the invidious (and exegetically questionable) task of defining the image of God in terms of some intrinsic property, which particular individuals may or may not possess. If the *imago Dei* refers not to some *thing* within us, but to some *one* outside of us, then we are freed from trying to justify our status through the critical examination of others or ourselves. What matters is our relationship with Jesus as the decisive common factor in our lives as human persons.

The problem is that this foundational relationship seems to be one in which Jesus disappears as a concrete individual and becomes little more than a pointer to the personhood of others. It is correspondingly hard to see how our own integrity as persons is bound up with our relationship to him in his particularity as the incarnate Word of God, or, indeed, that it is possible to have a relationship with him at all.

If these implications are to be avoided, it must be made clear that Jesus points us to others not because he lacks a particular identity of his own, but rather, because his identity resists homogenization. That the risen Christ has ascended to the right hand of God gives him this stability, because his absence from our history, if taken seriously, undercuts every attempt to use him to define the boundaries of human personhood. Thus, if his resurrection displaces his identity in a way that exposes the occlusion of the other, his ascension proclaims that his identity (and that of the rest of us) is not thereby dissolved in a shifting array of signifiers, but rather, is hidden with God. As such, it provides the focal point in reference to which our identities are defined, but the discontinuity between this focal point and our own identities subverts every attempt to make either Jesus or those for whom he came conform to our established notions of what a person is.

Therefore, having suggested that we are enabled to see others as persons only by reference to Jesus, I now must explore in greater detail what this christological framework implies for our acknowledging of others as persons. After all, while rocks, trees, and nebulae are also not Jesus, we don't attribute personhood to them. Given the Christian conviction that Jesus is the one in whom all things are reconciled (Col. 1:20; cf. Eph. 1:10), it is necessary to explain how the relationship to us through which Jesus claims us as persons differs from his relationship to the rest of creation. Filling in that content is the task of the rest of this book, beginning in the next chapter with an exploration of the theological roots of the term "person."

- 3 -

The Concept of the Person
in Theological Perspective

An obvious response to the question of what distinguishes our relationship to Jesus from that of other creatures is that Jesus was himself a human being and not a horse or a fungus. This answer, however, only raises the further question of why theological anthropology needs the concept of person in the first place. Why not simply speak of human beings? After all, specifying what it means to be human is likely to prove no more complicated than defining "person" and would have the ancillary effect of limiting the proliferation of technical terms.

One way of responding to this challenge would be to refer once again to the colloquial sense in which our categorization of others as persons, though doubtless connected with our humanity in some way, refers to a value we assign them that is not simply identical to their membership in a particular species. From this perspective, to be treated like a person is not simply—or even primarily—to have a given biological identity, but to be acknowledged as having the right to expect, for example, the preservation of one's physical and psychological integrity, respect for one's freedom of action, and a claim on the attention of others.[1]

And yet to define personhood in terms like these could easily be taken to imply that all who for whatever reason cannot communicate, whose freedom of action is limited, or whose ability to make decisions is impaired are not persons in the full sense of the word. In this context, it is small wonder that some have questioned whether "person" is a particularly useful category when reflecting on our status

---

1. Something like this perspective underlies the arguments for the personhood of certain nonhuman mammals in Peter Singer, *Practical Ethics* (Cambridge: Cambridge University Press, 1979), ch. 5.

as creatures before God.[2] Given that one looks in vain in scripture for the kind of technical use of the term "person" characteristic of modern philosophical and theological discussion, Christians in particular might be thought to have good reason to give serious consideration to such counsel. Over against these suspicions, however, it is the burden of this chapter to argue that there are good theological reasons for assigning "person" a central role in Christian reflection on human being, the most important being that the term plays an important role in the Christian confession of Jesus as savior.

THE THEOLOGICAL ROOTS OF THE CONCEPT OF THE PERSON

Needless to say, if the term "person" is to be granted a central role in theological anthropology in spite of the absence of any equivalent in biblical Hebrew or Greek, a case needs to be made that it illumines some aspect of the biblical understanding of human being. As already noted, one way in which the distinctiveness of humankind is highlighted in scripture is by way of the claim that it is the only creature made in God's image (Gen. 1:26–27; cf. 5:1).[3] While the meaning of this phrase remains unexplored in the Old Testament, it acquires special significance in the New, where Jesus is explicitly identified as the image of God (2 Cor. 4:4; Col. 1:15), so that the salvation he brings can be described as a matter of our being restored (Col. 3:10) or conformed (Rom. 8:29; cf. 1 Cor. 15:49) to his image.[4] From this perspective, Jesus is the touchstone for any claims about the ultimate character of human being. It follows that if human beings are to be described as persons, it will be because the term applies first and foremost to Jesus.

As it happens, the use of the term "person" in theology can be seen as a consequence (albeit a rather indirect one) of early Christian reflection on this identification of Jesus with the divine image. The

---

2. See, e.g., Stanley Hauerwas, "Must a Patient Be a Person to Be a Patient? Or, My Uncle Charlie Is Not Much of a Person but He Is Still My Uncle Charlie," in *Truthfulness and Tragedy: Further Investigations in Christian Ethics* (Notre Dame, Ind.: Notre Dame University Press, 1977), 127–31.

3. For other references to humanity's place in the created order, see Genesis 2, Psalm 8, and (albeit in a less confident vein) Job 7:17; but cf. Eccl. 3:19.

4. See Thomas Aquinas, *Summa Theologiae*, Ia, q. 93, art. 1.

characterization of Jesus as God's image seems to be related to certain terminological developments in the intertestamental literature, where the phrase "image of God" is applied to the figure of divine Wisdom. Already in the Old Testament, Wisdom appears as a distinct aspect or manifestation of the divine being who is active alongside God in the work of creation (see Prov. 8:22–31). In the later Wisdom of Solomon, she is conceived as a sort of mediator between God and creation and, in this capacity, is described as "an image of [God's] goodness" (Wis. 7:26).[5] Jesus himself is identified explicitly with divine Wisdom in 1 Cor. 1:24 (cf. Matt. 11:19; Luke 11:49), and the affirmation in Colossians that "all things were created in him...through him and to him, and he is before all things, and all things are sustained in him" (Col. 1:16–17) also seems to reflect earlier descriptions of Wisdom as the agent of creation (see, e.g., Wis. 7:22).

But if the New Testament succeeds in giving definite historical form and content to the somewhat shadowy figure of Wisdom by identifying Jesus with the image of God, this move raises questions about the character of Jesus' relation to God. As the one described not only as the "reflection of God's glory and the exact imprint of God's very being," but also as "Son," Jesus is evidently superior to the angels (Heb. 1:3–14). But is he therefore equal with God? The witness of the New Testament writers seems ambiguous at first glance (John 1:1; 10:30; 20:28; but cf. Mark 10:18; John 14:28), and it was not until the fourth century, when faced with Arius's claim that the Word made flesh was a creature, that the Council of Nicea explicitly declared that the Word (or Son) who became incarnate was "of the same essence" (*homoousios*) as the God whom Jesus called Father. But even this definition did not solve the problem of Jesus' relationship to God, because it remained unclear how it was possible to affirm that the Father and the Son shared the same essence without either rendering them indistinguishable or, worse, implying that Christians worshiped two gods instead of one.

These parallel threats were answered through a terminological innovation that entailed distinguishing the Father, Son, and Spirit as a Trinity of three "persons" sharing one divine essence. Each person

---

5. See also Philo of Alexandria's descriptions of Wisdom (or Logos) as the divine image in *Legum allegoria* 1.43 and *De confusione linguarum* 146–47 (in *Philo*, 10 vols., Loeb Classical Library [London: William Heinemann, 1929–62], vols. 1 and 4).

was understood to be truly distinct from the other two (and thus not simply a more or less transient manifestation of some underlying divine reality) and yet inseparable from them in life and action (so that the three persons are not three gods in the way that Peter, Paul, and Mary are three independently subsisting human beings).[6] From this specifically trinitarian perspective, the justification of Christians' confession of Jesus as Savior lies in the fact that he is one of these persons. Of course, the term "person" was not invented for this purpose, and the consolidation of trinitarian language was complicated somewhat by the fact that the Greek theologians who hammered out the orthodox form of the doctrine shied away from the word *prosopon* (the Greek cognate of the Latin *persona*) in favor of the philosophically more respectable *hypostasis*. Terminological variations aside, however, the trinitarian controversy established that the Father, Son, and Spirit were not to be understood as masklike modifications of some ontologically more fundamental divine nature, but rather as that most basic reality which gives the divine nature its specific form.[7]

In short, while in ancient Greek thought the category of essence or nature was primary, the trinitarian controversy of the fourth century led Christians to the conclusion that the concept of person was primary. Father, Son, and Spirit were not names for variations or modes of some primordial divine essence, but were in fact constitutive of that essence. It is therefore not owing to the properties of an impersonal (or prepersonal) divine nature that God is God; rather, God's divinity is a function of the relationships between the three persons.[8] Put in other words, "God" does not so much name a particular kind of being as a communion of persons whose existence is characterized by the qualities of simplicity, unity, omnipotence, omniscience, and the like.

---

6. "But though we take it for granted that there are three persons and names, we do not imagine . . . three different lives. . . . Rather is it the same life which is produced by the Father, prepared by the Son, and depends on the will of the Holy Spirit" (Gregory of Nyssa, "An Answer to Ablabius: That We Should Not Think of Saying That There Are Three Gods," in *Christology of the Later Fathers*, ed. Edward R. Hardy [Philadelphia: Westminster, 1954], 262).

7. "The person is no longer an adjunct to a being, a category which we *add* to a concrete entity once we have first verified its ontological hypostasis. *It is itself the hypostasis of the being*" (John D. Zizioulas, *Being as Communion: Studies in Personhood and the Church* [Crestwood, N.Y.: St. Vladimir's Seminary Press, 1985], 39).

8. "Thus God as person . . . makes the one divine substance to be that which it is: the one God" (ibid., 41).

Trinitarian doctrine thus addresses the question of Jesus' (and, by
extension, the Holy Spirit's) relationship to God by arguing that God's
oneness is not an abstract or undifferentiated singleness, but a living
unity defined by the communion of three fully and equally divine "persons." Insofar as God is none other than these three in their triunity,
the persons are not to be conceived as independent entities; rather,
they coinhere in each other in such a way that each is equally the
subject of every divine act. Because talk about any one of the persons
entails talk about the other two, it is impossible to define what a person is in or by itself.[9] Trinitarian personhood is therefore characterized
by the loving commitment of each one to the other two rather than
by autonomy or self-sufficiency.[10] Indeed, to speak of the "person"
within a trinitarian context is not to define some (generic) *thing*, but
to identify some (concrete) *one* by reference to her or his relationships
to other, equally concrete someones.[11]

JESUS AS A PERSON

The modern Western concept of the person derives from these trinitarian roots.[12] Obviously, the primary application of the term "person"
to God does not render its use in the human sphere illegitimate, but
it does require that any such use be shown to be consistent with the
term's primary reference to the Father, Son, and Holy Spirit. In other
words, the theological ascription of the term to human beings needs
to be governed by what we are given to know of God rather than by
what we imagine we know of ourselves.

We may begin by pointing out that if "person" is predicated most
properly of the Father, Son, and Holy Spirit, then it cannot be defined
in terms of the possession of certain shared qualities or characteristics.
After all, that which the divine persons have in common is precisely

9. "The definition of divine persons as relations of origin means that to be a person
is to be defined by where a person comes from; *what a person is in itself or by itself cannot
be determined*" (Catherine Mowry LaCugna, *God for Us: The Trinity and Christian Life* [San
Francisco: HarperSanFrancisco, 1991], 69).

10. Ibid., 289. Cf. Wolfhart Pannenberg, *Systematic Theology*, vol. 1 (Grand Rapids:
Eerdmans, 1991), 426–27, 430.

11. In the words of the medieval theologian Richard of St. Victor, a person is "an in-
communicable existence of the divine nature" ("*divinae naturae incommunicabilis existentia*")
(*De Trinitate* 4.22; cited in Aquinas, *Summa Theologiae*, Ia, q. 29, art. 3).

12. See the discussion of Boethius on pp. 7–10 above.

their divine nature (with its attendant qualities of omnipotence, omniscience, omnipresence, etc.), and it is not this shared nature that distinguishes them as persons. Quite the contrary, their personhood refers precisely to what they do *not* share.[13] As Vladimir Lossky has pointed out, where the persons of the Trinity are concerned, "the only common definition possible would be the impossibility of a common definition."[14] In short, to be a person is not to be a certain kind of thing (e.g., self-conscious, rational, or relational), but simply to be the Father, the Son, or the Holy Spirit. And what it is to be any of these three is describable only in terms of the particular relationships in which they stand with each other.

We are given to know something about these relationships through the life of Jesus of Nazareth, since Jesus himself is understood to be one of these three persons—the Son or Word—made flesh. As the stimulus for the emergence of the theological concept of the person in the first place, Jesus remains the key to understanding personhood as the one in and through whom God's triune life becomes visible in history. In any case, allowing the doctrine of the Trinity to guide our use of the term "person" reminds us that Jesus' status as a person has nothing to do with his satisfying some general criteria of "the personal," but is simply a function of his being one of the three divine persons.

But if Jesus' personhood is not reducible to any general *definition* of the personal, its content can nevertheless be *described* in terms of his relationship to the other persons of the Trinity. Jesus is, for example, the one given (John 3:16) or sent (John 4:34; 5:24, 30, 36, 37, and passim) by the Father, and to whom the Father has committed all judgment (John 5:22–27) and authority (Matt. 28:18; cf. John 3:35; 13:3; 1 Cor. 15:24–28). Likewise, he is the one who is equipped to minister (Matt. 3:16–17 and pars.) and is raised (Rom. 1:4) by the power of the Spirit, and to whose sovereignty the Spirit bears witness (John 15:26; 1 Cor. 12:3; 1 John 4:2). This kind of description does not amount to a definition of personhood, since the Father and the Spirit are equally persons even though they do not relate to Jesus in

---

13. See Karl Rahner, *The Trinity* (New York: Herder and Herder, 1970), 104–5.
14. Vladimir Lossky, *In the Image and Likeness of God* (Crestwood, N.Y.: St. Vladimir's Seminary Press, 1985), 113.

the same way Jesus relates to them. At the same time, however, that the personhood of the Father, Son, and Spirit is inseparable from their standing in mutually constitutive, albeit diverse, relationships with one another seems to rule out the possibility of the term "person" being predicated of creatures.

And yet closer attention to the particular form of Jesus' personhood suggests that it may be possible to conceive of non-divine persons. Jesus himself declares that his mission as the Son sent from the Father is continued in the mission of the disciples whom he, in his turn, sends forth: "Whoever welcomes you welcomes me, and whoever welcomes me welcomes the one who sent me" (Matt. 10:40; cf. Mark 9:37; Luke 9:48; 10:16; John 12:44–45; 17:18). In a manner analogous to Jesus' representation of the one he calls Father, the disciples represent Jesus in and to the world as this Father's "Son." By entrusting his disciples with the ministry that identifies him as the second person of the Trinity, Jesus effectively calls them to share in the life of the Trinity in a way that identifies them as persons.

If the possibility of human personhood is understood to depend on Jesus treating people in a particular way, it follows that the disciples' status as persons does not depend on any specific qualities they possess. Their personhood rests entirely on their election by Jesus.[15] As persons, they are commissioned to represent Jesus in the same way that Jesus represents the God he calls Father, but their personhood is not constituted by their fidelity to this mission. It is established instead by the fact of Jesus' representing them before God as friends (John 15:13–15), for whom he prays (John 17:9; cf. Luke 22:31–32) and consecrates himself (John 17:19), so that they might join the communion he shares as a person with the Father (John 17:21, 26). This theme is taken up and developed in the Epistle to the Hebrews, where Jesus is described as a priest who is able to intercede on our behalf before God (2:17; cf. 4:15; 6:20; 1 John 2:1). If Christ is a person because he is the Son, then we are persons insofar as Christ intercedes for us by claiming us as fellow sons and daughters of the Father. In the words of Hans Urs von Balthasar, "This Jesus is a person. Others

---

15. "It is impossible to become a person except by becoming a brother of the 'First-born'" (Hans Urs von Balthasar, *Dramatis Personae: Persons in Christ*, vol. 3 of *Theo-Drama: Theological Dramatic Theory*, trans. Graham Harrison [San Francisco: Ignatius, 1992], 249).

can claim to be persons only in virtue of a relationship with him and in dependence on him."[16]

REPRESENTATION AND SUBSTITUTION

Is this way of understanding human personhood consistent with the commitment to the integrity of the other that was placed at the core of Jesus' identity in chapter 2? There it was argued that the chief threat to personhood is the process of occlusion in which the other is neither acknowledged nor accepted as a person in her own right. Instead, she is either regarded as fundamentally the same as oneself, or, to the extent that her difference from oneself is recognized, her full personhood is questioned. Doesn't the thesis that we are persons only by virtue of Jesus' intercession for us constitute just such a process of occlusion, since we appear to count as persons only to the extent that our individual distinctiveness is subsumed under (and thus hidden behind) that of Jesus?

It is with concerns of this sort in mind that Dorothee Sölle has insisted on the need to conceive of Christ's work on our behalf as a matter of representation rather than substitution. A substitute, she notes, displaces someone and thereby renders that person superfluous; consequently, a Jesus who is our substitute leaves us no place before God. Insofar as Jesus comes precisely to secure us such a place, Sölle argues that he is more accurately conceived as our representative (Stellvertreter, literally "placeholder").[17] While a substitute implicitly undermines our distinctiveness by taking our place, a representative affirms it by keeping a place open for us.[18]

Sölle maintains that Christ's status as our representative must be conceived as provisional, on the grounds that genuine representation anticipates the time when the person for whom a place is held will be able to occupy it in her or his own right.[19] When representation

---

16. Ibid., 207. Cf. Karl Barth, Church Dogmatics [hereafter CD], 13 vols., ed. G. W. Bromiley and T. F. Torrance (Edinburgh: Clark, 1956–74), III/2, 135: "the ontological determination of all men is that Jesus is present among them as their divine Other, their Neighbour, Companion and Brother."

17. Dorothee Sölle, Christ the Representative: An Essay in Theology after the "Death of God" (London: SCM, 1967), 103–4.

18. Ibid., 55.

19. Ibid., 105; cf. 107–12.

is permanent, she argues, it ceases to be representation and becomes substitution, in which the effective replacement of the one "represented" makes it impossible to affirm that she or he has irreplaceable value before God. Although Sölle's position diverges sharply from the idea (on which the Reformers in particular insisted) that human beings are never able to hold their own before God apart from Christ, it does pose the question of how Christ's ministry of representing us before God can be permanent without making our own presence redundant.

Sölle's discussion of the relationship between substitution and representation reflects modern concerns about the value of the individual, but the issues she raises echo far older concerns about Christ's relationship to us. The christological debates of the church's early centuries were also driven by the need to clarify what had to be true about Jesus if his work was to be defended as the salvation and not the occlusion or annihilation of other human beings. Clearly, if Jesus were the unique Savior of the human race, he could not be captive to sin in the same way that the rest of us were; at the same time (as suggested by biblical passages like Gal. 4:4–5 and Heb. 2:14–18), it would be impossible for him to intercede for us if he were not like us. How are these demands for similarity and difference to be reconciled?

The issue of Jesus' distinctiveness was largely settled with the formal definition of orthodox trinitarianism at the Council of Constantinople in 381, where the Word made flesh was defined as one of three consubstantial divine persons, each equal in divinity to the other two. By contrast, articulating Jesus' likeness to the rest of humankind proved a more intractable problem. Gregory of Nazianzus (who had played a significant role in working out the trinitarian language adopted at Constantinople) established a touchstone for subsequent debate by arguing that Jesus could redeem the whole human person only if he himself were fully human.[20] This principle acquired dogmatic status in 451, when the Council of Chalcedon confirmed that Christ was consubstantial (*homoousios*) with humankind as well as with God; but assent to the principle that Jesus was fully human as well as fully divine did not translate into agreement on how these two natures were

---

20. "That which he has not assumed he has not healed; but that which is united to his Godhead is also saved" ("To Cledonius the Priest against Apollinarius," in Ep. CI, *Cyril of Jerusalem, Gregory Nazianzen*, vol. 7 of *The Nicene and Post-Nicene Fathers*, 2nd series, ed. Philip Schaff and Henry Wace [Peabody, Mass.: Hendrickson, 1995 (1894)], 440).

united in him. Specifically, it was unclear whether Christ, insofar as he was confessed to be consubstantial both with God and with mankind, should be described as one person or two. Either alternative posed serious problems: the former option seemed to suggest that in Jesus divinity and humanity had been blended into some third substance, while the latter risked the specter of two parallel Christs, with the divine Word shadowing the human being Jesus.

The christological formula adopted at Chalcedon addressed this issue by declaring that while the divine and human *natures* in Christ retained their separate integrity (having been joined "without confusion, without change"), they nevertheless subsisted as a single person, or hypostasis (since they were united "without division, without separation"). This "hypostatic union" between the divine and human natures meant that Jesus' various experiences were not to be divided up between his divinity and humanity, but were simply to be attributed to Jesus Christ as the one Word made flesh. In this way, the force of the Chalcedonian formula was grammatical rather than metaphysical: rather than try to explain how divinity and humanity were united in Christ, the Council simply decreed that to identify Jesus was to identify the divine Word, and, likewise, that the Word was identified by pointing to Jesus.[21]

A review of the objections raised against the Chalcedonian formula is beyond the scope of the present study, but even the Council's defenders soon recognized that the claim that Jesus was just one hypostasis raised the question of what kind of hypostasis he was. In the course of the trinitarian controversy, "hypostasis" had come to be defined as the particular instantiation of a nature, so that, for example, Peter and Paul constitute distinct human hypostases, and the persons of the Trinity could be characterized as divine hypostases. Since Chalcedonians worked initially under the presupposition that a nature could be present only if instantiated in a distinct hypostasis, defenders of the Council had to explain how it was possible to say that Christ had two natures if one of them was "anhypostatic" (i.e., without a corresponding hypostasis).

Inasmuch as the Councils of Nicea and Constantinople had af-

---

21. Eric W. Gritsch and Robert W. Jenson, *Lutheranism: The Theological Movement and Its Confessional Writings* (Philadelphia: Fortress, 1976), 93–94.

firmed that the Word that became flesh was the second person of
the Trinity, it was a matter of consensus in the Chalcedonian church
that the one hypostasis of Jesus Christ was divine.[22] It followed that
Christ's human nature had no corresponding human hypostasis of its
own. On a grammatical level, this conclusion merely reaffirmed the
point that Jesus' identity was that of the Word; but in light of the
metaphysical assumption that a nature could only be said to be present
if it was "hypostasized," the idea that Christ lacked a human hypostasis appeared to undermine the claim that he had a fully human
nature.[23] How could Jesus be fully human if he lacked a concrete
human identity?

In answering this question, the trinitarian ontology developed by
the Cappadocians proved helpful. As already noted, the Cappadocians argued that within the Godhead the three divine persons (or
hypostases) were ontologically prior to the divine essence or nature:[24]
God is not first an undifferentiated essence that is subsequently divided into hypostatically distinct persons; rather, the divine essence is
a manifestation of the freedom of the persons of the Trinity in relation.
It is this ontological priority of the hypostasis over the nature that distinguishes the three divine hypostases as "persons" in the trinitarian
sense. Individual creatures, whether humans in a city or roses on a
bush, are also distinct hypostases, but they do not exhibit the combination of mutuality and freedom characteristic of the divine persons:
we can conceive of Paul without Peter, and of human being in general
without either of them; by contrast, we cannot conceive of the Father

---

22. For a review of the search for a conceptual framework capable of supporting this
conclusion, see Aloys Grillmeier, *Christ in Christian Tradition*, vol. 2.2 (London: Mowbray,
1995), 186–89, 277–82, 437–38.

23. Grillmeier (ibid., 284) points out that even staunch Chalcedonians feared that to
characterize Christ's human nature as anhypostatic was equivalent to declaring it unreal.

24. Technically, the trinitarian controversy turned on the distinction between hypostasis and essence (*ousia*), and the christological controversy on that between hypostasis
and nature (*physis*). But while the distinction between essence and nature was important
for certain Christologies developed after 451, the two terms tended to be functionally
synonymous among Chalcedonians, for whom the decisive issue was the conceptual priority of hypostasis with respect to essence and nature alike. Thus, by the eighth century,
one Orthodox writer saw no problem in affirming that "ousia and nature [*physis*] are the
same" (Anastasius, *Doctrina patrum de incarnatione Verbi*, 6.1; cited in Jaroslav Pelikan, *The
Spirit of Eastern Christendom (600–1700)*, vol. 2 of *The Christian Tradition: A History of the
Development of Doctrine* [Chicago: University of Chicago Press, 1974], 81).

without the Son, or of God apart from the particularity of Father, Son, and Spirit.

The idea that the hypostasis is properly conceived as the active source rather than a derivative of the divine nature could also be deployed to answer the question of how two natures could be joined in the single, personal hypostasis of the Word. The solution lay in distinguishing the principle that a nature could not subsist without *some* individuating hypostasis from the claim that every subsisting nature had to have a *separate* hypostasis.[25] Because the trinitarian hypostases are ontologically prior to the divine nature, they are not limited or restricted by it. The Word is therefore free to adopt a human nature without any loss of divinity.[26] Correspondingly, the claim that the human nature assumed by the Word lacked a human hypostasis does not force the conclusion that it has no hypostatic instantiation at all; instead, it can be argued that the human nature subsists within the hypostasis of the divine Word.

In this way, the Word's taking flesh extends the priority of person over nature characteristic of the Trinity to the human sphere: human nature is reconfigured as a manifestation of personal freedom (specifically, the freedom of the second person of the Trinity) rather than a set of ontologically given constraints on individual existence. God in Christ thereby opens human nature to "personal" existence in the specifically trinitarian sense of "sharing in the mutual love of the Father, Son, and Spirit." Moreover, the anhypostatic character of Jesus' human nature means that the Word makes space for human beings to exist as persons without filling that space in a way that would displace or occlude the particularity of other human beings. John Meyendorff puts it as follows:

> God assumed humanity in a way which did not exclude any human hypostasis, but which opened to all of them the possibility of restoring their unity in [God]. [God] became, indeed, the

---

25. In other words, hypostasis could be characterized as "the personal, 'acting' *source* of natural life; but...not 'nature,' or life itself" (John Meyendorff, *Byzantine Theology: Historical Trends and Doctrinal Themes* [New York: Fordham University Press, 1974], 154).

26. "The distinction between substance and hypostasis in the Trinity...is a way of indicating that the hypostasis of the Word...is not restricted to its own substance or nature. Without loss to itself, it may therefore take on a created nature" (Kathryn Tanner, "Who Is Jesus? Christological Conundrums," unpublished MS of the *Scottish Journal of Theology Lectures,* 1999).

"new Adam," in whom every [human being] finds his [or her] own nature realized perfectly and fully, without the limitations which would have been inevitable if Jesus were only a human personality.[27]

In other words, the incarnation is not the election of the particular man Jesus as a person to the exclusion of all other human beings, but rather the election of all human beings to be persons in and through the particular man Jesus.

Yet this way of understanding Christ's work of representation has two outstanding problems. First, the suggestion that Jesus establishes human nature as a hypostatically open space that we *can* fill seems to imply that there comes a point where we *need to assume responsibility* for filling it—a possibility at odds with the principle that our acceptance by God is at no point conditional on our own merits or abilities. Second, when Christ's role is defined as the essentially passive one of not taking our place, our own particularity as human persons seems to be secured at the price of obscuring Jesus' human particularity: by confessing Jesus' humanity as anhypostatic, we seem to reduce it to an ontologically empty space. According to the witness of the Johannine literature in particular, love characterizes the relationship of the divine persons with one another and with ourselves; but how can we either love or be loved by someone whose personhood is seemingly detached from his flesh-and-blood existence?

These difficulties can be resolved only by providing a fuller account of Christ's person. If human beings remain permanently incapable of securing a place before God, then clearly, Christ's work as our representative must involve something more than the negative condition of not taking our place before God. It is certainly important that Christ leaves us space to be persons; but for this part of his work to be of any use to us, he must also actively and effectively secure that space for us. While the claim that Jesus' human nature is anhypostatic is a necessary condition of our being able to be counted as persons, it is not sufficient, since it does no good for Christ to leave us space before God unless he also makes it possible for us to occupy it. The question is how our occupying that space can be said to depend on Christ's presence for us without rendering our own presence redundant.

---

27. Meyendorff, *Byzantine Theology*, 159.

PERSONHOOD AND REPRESENTATION

As already noted, the point of the doctrine of the anhypostasis was to affirm that the divine Word was Jesus' sole and entire identity. By defining Jesus' human nature as anhypostatic, the church made it clear that the second person of the Trinity did not take the flesh of an independently existing human being, but rather, became man by assuming human nature. In other words, the fact that Jesus' human nature was anhypostatic did not mean that it lacked any hypostasis at all, but that it had one divine hypostasis as its identity. Thus, at the same time that his human nature was declared to lack a separate human hypostasis, it was affirmed to have been "enhypostasized" by (and therefore to be "enhypostatic" in) the divine hypostasis of the Word. In this way, the category of enhypostasis complemented that of anhypostasis by affirming the concrete particularity of Jesus' human life over against any suggestion that his humanity was featureless or generic.

In order to explain the significance of this point for our existence as persons, it is necessary to be more precise about what it means to say that our personhood derives from Jesus representing us as persons before God. Etymologically, to "re-present" is to make present. One represents a tree, for example, by painting a picture of it or writing a poem about it; while the tree itself may not be at hand, it is made present—and thus made known as the particular tree it is—for the one seeing the picture or reading the poem. In a specifically social context, representation describes the work of standing in for another as her or his official (in the sense of publicly recognized) proxy. For example, an attorney represents his client in a court of law; and, on a larger scale, a Senator represents her constituents in Congress.

The scope of a representative's activity depends on the setting. In a rehearsal for a graduation ceremony, for example, someone may be chosen to represent the keynote speaker in the procession or on the dais. Such a "representative" need have no personal knowledge whatsoever of the one being represented; he merely marks her place in the ceremony. The scope of representation is greater in a legislative context. While the legislator may be personally acquainted with only a tiny fraction of her constituency, she nevertheless will need to possess a general sense of their interests in order to represent them effectively.

Moving still further along the spectrum, a defense attorney in a capital case requires a detailed knowledge of his client if he is to represent her competently.

Though the comprehensive character of Jesus' representation of us before God leads one biblical writer to understand his role as analogous to that of an attorney (John 14:16; cf. 1 John 2:1), Christians have interpreted his work of representation as involving a far greater degree of identification with us than that of even the most dedicated trial lawyer. Because Jesus does not merely speak for us, but actually sacrifices himself on our behalf, many Christians have followed the lead of the writer of Hebrews (see especially Heb. 9:24–26; cf. 2 Cor. 5:21) in interpreting his activity after the model of a priest.[28] The difference lies in the fact that a priest does not simply defend the "client's" interests, but actually effects reconciliation between the estranged parties. Jesus' work is priestly insofar as he accomplishes the work of reconciliation with God that the Levitical priesthood of the Old Testament could only foreshadow. His intercession does not convince God of our acceptability (as though God needed to be made more fully aware of the facts of our situation); it actually renders us acceptable (1 Cor. 1:30; cf. Rom. 8:34).

As our (priestly) representative, Jesus creates the conditions under which we are acknowledged by God as persons in the trinitarian sense that Jesus is. Jesus thus represents us to God as his "fellow heirs" (Rom. 8:17), whom he is "not ashamed" to call sisters and brothers (Heb. 2:11). "Justification" is the term traditionally used to characterize this work in Christian theology, but insofar as its content is that God acknowledges us as "fellow heirs" with Christ and "children" alongside the only-begotten Son, in the present context it might as well be termed "personalization." In any event, the claim that we are "justified" (or "personalized") as a direct result of Jesus representing us before God can be elaborated in terms of two related principles. First, to attribute our justification to Jesus is to deny that human beings are acceptable in God's sight (i.e., that God treats them as persons) apart from Jesus' mediation. In this sense, justification is, to use the

---

28. See, for example, John Calvin, *Institutes of the Christian Religion*, ed. John T. McNeill (Philadelphia: Westminster, 1960), II.15, and Friedrich Schleiermacher, *The Christian Faith*, ed. H. R. Mackintosh and J. S. Stewart (Edinburgh: Clark, 1928), §104. Cf. Barth, CD, IV/1, 135.

language of classical Lutheranism, "forensic," meaning that our acceptability (or righteousness) is imputed to us for Jesus' sake and is not a quality we possess on our own account. We are not justified (or "personalized") because we are worthy; rather, we are worthy because we have been justified.

At the same time, however (and this is the second point), insofar as human beings are seen by God as acceptable "in Christ," they truly *are* acceptable. A parallel may be drawn here with the event of creation. Even as the world must be confessed as genuinely good because God saw it as good at the time of its creation (Gen. 1:4, 10, 12, 18, 25, 31), so in the work of redemption God's seeing us as persons in Christ means that we are genuinely persons. Because our status as persons depends entirely on our being in Christ, it is not something we can boast about as our own possession; but neither is it the case that God's seeing us as persons is arbitrary, as though God might just as easily see us in a different way. God's seeing, in redemption no less than in creation, is understood to be right and fitting, though the truth of what is seen cannot be separated from the act of God's seeing it. Because we are not persons (defined, once again, as sharers in the trinitarian communion of persons) apart from what God has done in Christ, an individual human being's personhood is visible only as one "sees" with God by refusing to look at her or him apart from Christ.[29]

PERSONHOOD AND WITNESS

As our representative before God, Jesus does far more than define a hypostatically open space for us to occupy through our own efforts. Nor does his work consist in relating the facts of our situation to God in the fashion of an impartial observer. After all, it is a central conviction of Christian belief that such objectivity would only confirm our guilt as creatures that have willfully turned away from God. In representing us, Jesus intercedes on our behalf before God in a way that actually changes the facts of our situation. Jesus constitutes us as persons by putting us in the place he holds open for us.

One way to understand this process is by comparison with the practice of bearing witness in a court of law. The testimony of a character

29. See pp. 74–75.

witness in the sentencing phase of a trial provides an analogy to the idea of a third party confirming someone as a person in the eyes of another, thereby rendering her justified in a way that she would not be apart from that witness. For example, the purpose of bringing the mother of a convicted murderer to testify is not primarily to disclose new facts about the life of the guilty party. To be sure, a mother put on the stand will undoubtedly relate a great many such facts, but that is not the point of her testimony. What she has to say in no way changes the defendant's guilt. Its aim is rather to encourage the jury to "see" the defendant in a new way—as a person whom they have the responsibility to treat *as* a person, in spite of the evil that the defendant has done. Moreover, such witness is unique and irreplaceable: only the mother is in a position to "personalize" her child in this particular way; she alone is in a position to establish that person as her son or daughter.

The idea that our status as persons is bound up with the witness given by another has certain affinities with relational models of personhood. Instead of focusing on our role in establishing and maintaining relationships, however (a strategy that renders the personhood of comatose, psychotic, and other mentally impaired persons problematic), the category of witness emphasizes the extrinsic character of our personhood by highlighting its dependence on the relation that someone else (viz., Jesus Christ) assumes with respect to us, regardless of the level or quality with which we reciprocate. The idea that I come to conceive myself as a person because other human beings treat me as such also has some psychological plausibility: if all those around me suddenly ceased to treat me like a person, I think it likely that I would start to doubt my personhood. Faced with forces attempting to erode my sense of personhood in the present, my ability to maintain some sense of myself as a person in such circumstances would in all likelihood depend on my experience of having been treated like a person in the past.[30]

The problem, of course, is that the testimony other human beings might give to our personhood can never be more than partial: no human being has the comprehensive knowledge of the totality of

---

30. Primo Levi argues that life in the Nazi death camps approximated to just such a situation. See his *Survival in Auschwitz: The Nazi Assault on Humanity* (New York: Collier, 1995), and *The Drowned and the Saved*, ed. Erroll McDonald (New York: Vintage, 1989).

another's existence that would be necessary to establish her or his personhood. For example, however powerful a mother's witness to her child may be, it is incapable of shedding much light on her child's identity as a spouse or parent. Moreover, even if someone had the kind of comprehensive knowledge necessary to illuminate every aspect of another's identity, the fact that this potential witness has her own specific hypostatic identity means that she could not fully represent another without effectively annihilating herself as a distinct person in her own right, and thereby subverting the value of her testimony as the witness of an "other."

Dostoyevsky gave classic formulation to these inherent limits on human witness in Ivan Karamazov's story of a peasant woman forced to watch her son hunted down and killed by the local landowner's hounds:

> I do not want a mother to embrace the torturer who had her child torn to pieces by his dogs! If she likes, she can forgive him for herself, she can forgive the torturer for the immeasurable suffering he has inflicted upon her as a mother; but she has no right to forgive him for the sufferings of her tortured child. She has no right to forgive the torturer for that, even if her child were to forgive him![31]

The problem Ivan identifies is twofold. First, any one person's witness to another is only partial; second, it is nontransferable. So while the mother in the story can forgive the torturer for the wrong done to her, she cannot forgive him for the wrong done to her child. No one but the child can affirm his relationship with the torturer in the face of the evil the latter has committed against him. From Ivan's perspective, even God does not have the right to forgive the torturer, because God did not suffer the wrong.

Of course, it is Dostoyevsky's contention that Ivan is wrong: God does have the right to forgive and exercises it through the intercession of Jesus Christ. The question is how appeal to Jesus can escape the inherent limitations of human witness. Ivan's challenge allows that our being affirmed as persons can avoid the charge of "cheap grace"

---

31. Fyodor Dostoyevsky, *The Brothers Karamazov*, vol. 1, trans. David Magarshack (London: Penguin, 1958), 287.

only if Jesus' witness to our personhood can transcend the partial and
fragmentary character of all merely human testimony. In the particular case of the torturer, this means that Jesus' witness must be able to
incorporate the standpoint of the victim, without depriving either the
victim or the torturer of his own integrity as a person. To the extent
that personhood is understood to entail an honoring of the person's
irreplaceable and unsubstitutable particularity, these conditions seemingly cannot be met. We are back at the problem of how a Jesus who
is concrete enough to constitute us as persons can do so in a way
that does not smother our personhood. The next chapter explores the
possibility of finding a way beyond this apparent impasse.

– 4 –

The Personhood
of Jesus Christ

Ivan Karamazov's story of the torturer challenges Christians to explain how God can sustain us as persons without betraying the integrity of our personhood. This challenge highlights an apparent contradiction in the account of personhood with which the last chapter ended: on the one hand, we can be vindicated as persons only by an act of witness that encompasses the whole of our lives; but on the other hand, any testimony sufficiently comprehensive to secure our identities would seem to threaten our uniqueness and irreplaceability as persons. In short, it appears that the unsubstitutability of persons is incompatible with the kind of absolute commitment to the other necessary to guarantee her or his existence as a person.

A possible solution to this dilemma is suggested by the biblical depiction of Jesus as a person whose identity is defined from beginning to end by his witness to the sovereignty of God (John 5:30; cf. 4:34; 6:38; Matt. 26:38–44 and pars.; Luke 23:46). Far from diminishing Jesus' distinctiveness, this unwavering commitment to the one he calls Father is precisely what establishes Jesus' identity as "Son."[1] Moreover, as our window onto the inner form of God's triune life, Jesus' story reveals that the same kind of commitment to the other that marks his relationship to the one he calls Father is characteristic of all the relationships between the divine persons. So, for example, Jesus' witness to the divinity of the Father is matched by the Father's witness to Jesus as the Son (Matt. 3:16–17; 17:5 and pars.; cf. John 5:37; 12:28) to whom all authority has been given (Matt. 28:18; John 5:22). Likewise,

---

1. See Wolfhart Pannenberg, *Systematic Theology*, vol. 1 (Edinburgh: Clark, 1989), 310–11.

alongside Jesus' witness to the Spirit as the one proceeding from the Father lies the Spirit's witness to Jesus as the one sent by the Father (John 15:26; cf. 16:14–15). Insofar as the Christian understanding of personhood takes its cue from this trinitarian prototype, it seems worthwhile to consider the possibility that radical identification with another is inconsistent neither with respecting that person's integrity nor with preserving one's own (cf. Matt. 10:39; 16:25 and pars.).

DIVINE PERSONHOOD REVISITED

All this is not to deny that care needs to be taken when translating the relations between the divine persons to the creaturely sphere. The degree to which the relationships between the persons of the Trinity provide a model for understanding what it means for human beings to be persons is limited. For example, it should not be supposed that the quality of "identification with another" could be abstracted from its trinitarian context and put forward as a criterion of personhood in general. To do so would be to fly in the face of the principle that there is no such thing as personhood "in general," since the term "person" refers specifically to the Father, Son, and Spirit. From this perspective, any attempt to define personhood in terms of "identification with another" opens the door to the same issues of individual capacity that mark traditional attempts to identify the personal with qualities like self-consciousness or rationality.

Thus, while Jesus remains the "point of contact" between divine personhood and our own, the role of the second person in shaping the inner life of the Trinity is not parallel to that of Jesus in establishing us as persons. The life of the Trinity is characterized by an ontological interdependence that is not a feature of Jesus' relationship with us. The Son receives his identity as Son from the Father; conversely, the Father receives his from the Son. By contrast, although we are persons solely by virtue of the fact that Jesus bears witness to us as persons before the Father, whatever witness we may bear to Jesus in return plays no role in establishing his personhood (John 5:34, 41). By taking flesh in Jesus, the second person establishes human nature as capable of bearing a personal hypostasis; but insofar as the term "person" applies properly to the divine hypostases alone, this "capacity" is absolutely dependent on the fact of the incarnation and cannot be considered a property of human nature apart from that event.

Importantly, the principle that the human has no inherent capacity for personal existence applies to Jesus' humanity no less than our own. By affirming that Jesus' status as a person is a result of the Word having assumed a fully human life, the principle of enhypostasis rules out any interpretation of personhood in terms of some intrinsic human characteristic or capacity. For while Jesus is confessed to have all such characteristics and capacities, he is not a person for that reason, but only because the Word has enhypostasized a human nature that is not personal in and of itself.

At the same time, however, the principle of enhypostasis should not be understood to imply that the Word directly determines Jesus' human activities,[2] since in that case Jesus could no longer be confessed as in every respect like those of us who are not incarnate members of the Trinity. If Jesus' consubstantiality with us is to be affirmed, then it follows that his human will, and not the divine Word, must have been in him "the immediate principle of all his moral operations, even as ours are in us."[3] But if the Word is not the immediate source of Jesus' human actions, what does it mean to say that Jesus is the Word? And how can the structure of his personhood be conceived in a way that allows other human beings to be conceived as persons too?

THE PNEUMATIC FORM
OF HUMAN PERSONHOOD

In answering these questions it is important to distinguish what makes us persons (or the *fact* of our personhood) from the concrete shape of our lives as persons (or its *form*). The first is a matter of God's unilateral act in Christ on our behalf; the second, of the life we lead in response to this act. The argument of this book is that we are persons because God treats us as such by speaking to us the same Word that

---

2. See Alan Spence, "Christ's Humanity and Ours: John Owen," in *Persons Divine and Human: King's College Essays in Theological Anthropology,* ed. Christoph Schwöbel and Colin E. Gunton (Edinburgh: Clark, 1991), 80–81.

3. John Owen, *A Discourse Concerning the Holy Spirit,* in *The Works of John Owen,* vol. 3, ed. W. H. Gould (London: Banner of Truth Trust, 1972 [1674]), 169. Cited in Spence, "Christ's Humanity and Ours," 83.

is constitutive of the personal life of the Trinity.[4] Yet if all human beings are persons because the Word is addressed to them, Jesus alone is the Word incarnate. For this reason, he is the only human being who is a person in his own right. In this respect, the fact of Jesus' personhood is unique. Nevertheless, there is no reason why the basic form of Jesus' life as a person in the Word cannot be repeated in other human beings; indeed, such a common structure must be assumed if Jesus' humanity is confessed to be the same as our own.

The figure who grounds this common form is the Holy Spirit. The Spirit's role in forming Jesus' life is well attested in scripture, where the Spirit is portrayed as active in the Word's incarnation (Matt. 1:18; Luke 1:35), as well as in the more decisive events of Jesus' earthly career (e.g., Matt. 3:16; 4:1; 12:28 and pars.; cf. Luke 4:18, 21; 10:21), culminating in the resurrection (Rom. 1:4; 1 Tim. 3:16; 1 Pet. 3:18). These passages together provide a strong basis for the claim that the life of the Word made flesh is constituted pneumatically. In other words, Jesus' identity as the incarnate Word is inseparable from the life he leads as a particular human being in the power of the Holy Spirit. In this way, it is by the Holy Spirit and not by the direct action of the Word that the human being Jesus lives the life of a person.

If the rest of humanity is to share in this basic form of human personhood, then (1) all human personhood must be a function of having been addressed by the Word, and (2) this address must be mediated by the Holy Spirit. Both these principles are consistent with the New Testament witness to the character of the life with God that Jesus makes possible for us. Certainly, there is no shortage of passages that depict the operation of the Spirit as crucial to our sharing Jesus' relationship with God (John 3:5–8; 7:38–39; Acts 10:44–47; 19:1–6; Gal. 4:6; Eph. 2:18; 1 John 3:24; 4:13; cf. Matt. 3:11 and pars.; Acts 11:16). In the same way that Jesus is vindicated as the Son of God in the power of the Spirit (Rom. 1:4), so for the rest of the human family those who are led by the Spirit of God are established as "sons" authorized to join with Jesus in calling God "Abba" (Rom. 8:14–16).

In Jesus' case no less than our own, then, human beings live as persons by virtue of the Word's pneumatically mediated address to

---

4. "If I ask: Who am I? . . . then if I understand myself in the light of God or His Word, I must answer that I am summoned by this Word, and to that extent I am in this Word" (Barth, *CD*, III/2, 150).

them. This means that life as a person necessarily involves reference to Jesus as the concrete form of the Word's existence in time and space. The difference between Jesus and the rest of us lies in the character of that reference: all human beings are addressed equally by the Word; but the Word comes to those of us who are not Jesus from outside ourselves, whereas in the case of Jesus, the Word's address is identical with his own life.[5]

In biblical understanding, the fact of the Word's address to us calls forth a response in the Spirit that takes the form of confession of Jesus as Lord (see, e.g., 1 Cor. 12:3; 1 John 4:2).[6] Once again, however, this does not mean that a human being's identity as a person (as opposed to the extent to which that identity is lived out) in any way depends on her or his witness to Jesus as God's Word. If it did, then personhood would once again be tied to a human capacity that might or might not be realized in any particular life. Scripture, however, makes it clear that our witness as human beings to the Word made flesh is a consequence rather than the cause of our relationship with that Word (see, e.g., 1 John 4:10–19).[7] But how is so apparently one-sided a relationship to be conceived in a way that does not define our personhood as so extrinsic to our being as to undermine the content of personal existence as participation in the trinitarian communion of God?

THE SOMATIC FORM
OF HUMAN PERSONHOOD

At several points in his correspondence, Paul describes Christians' relationship with Jesus in terms of their having been baptized "into"

---

5. Dietrich Bonhoeffer, *Christ the Center*, in *A Testament to Freedom: The Essential Writings of Dietrich Bonhoeffer*, ed. Geffrey B. Kelly and F. Burton Nelson (San Francisco: HarperSanFrancisco, 1990), 128: "because Jesus Christ *is* also God's judgment on himself, he points, at one and the same time, to both God and to himself." See the debate over the significance of Jesus' witness to himself in John 5:31–32; 8:12–18.

6. "Man is . . . as he . . . offer[s] himself as the response to the Word of God, and conducting, shaping and expressing himself as an answer to it" (Barth, *CD* III/2, 175).

7. According to Hans Urs von Balthasar, because human beings "are bearers of dramatic roles, a priori and intrinsically, even before they begin to act," whatever response they give is a matter of "becom[ing] what in God's sight they always have been" (Hans Urs von Balthasar, *Dramatis Personae: Persons in Christ*, vol. 3 of *Theo-Drama: Theological Dramatic Theory*, trans. Graham Harrison [San Francisco: Ignatius, 1992], 270).

him (Rom. 6:3; Gal. 3:27; cf. Acts 8:16; 19:5). He gives this rather cryptic image in a more concrete sense in 1 Corinthians 12:

> For just as the body is one and has many members, and all the members of the body, though many, are one body, so it is with Christ. For in the one Spirit we were all baptized into one body— Jews or Greeks, slaves or free—and we were all made to drink of one Spirit. (1 Cor. 12:12–13)

This passage consolidates many of the themes adumbrated in the previous section: Christians benefit from the same Spirit that was active in Jesus, and it is by virtue of this Spirit's activity that they share Jesus' life with God. And yet, while it remains true that the Spirit does not change us into Jesus, more is at stake than our being "like" him, or even our being transformed into his image. According to Paul, in being baptized into Christ, we become part of his body: "Now you are the body of Christ and individually members of it" (1 Cor. 12:27; cf. Rom. 12:4–5).

That Jesus Christ has a body is not generally a matter of contention in the modern era, but that this "body" is capable of including an indefinite number of other human beings as constituent members is not quite so easily taken for granted. Notwithstanding the difficult questions raised by the phenomenon of conjoined twins and the practices of abortion and organ transplantation, we tend to think of the boundaries of the human body as clearly defined. The customs and laws that govern our society operate on the principle that each human being has his or her own body. Indeed, the concept of "human rights" is largely understood in terms of the individual's ability to exercise control of his or her body free of interference from other bodies.

Of course, this physiological understanding of the body does not rule out a metaphorical use of the term—one as common in Paul's time as our own—in which a particular group (e.g., a family, the citizens of a town or nation, or some voluntary organization) speaks of itself as a "body" of which constituent individuals are "members." And yet Paul seems to be doing something more in his letters than recycling an established rhetorical trope. He does not tell the Roman and Corinthian Christians that they are "a" body in the general and more or less ill-defined way that any social group might be so conceived, but rather, that they are *the* body of *Christ*, and thus that they derive their identity from this particular human life. The relationship between Christ and his members thus has a form that is defined by the particularity of Jesus' career as the crucified and risen one. So, for example, Paul can speak of "always carrying in the body the death of Jesus, so that the life of Jesus may also be made visible in our bodies" (2 Cor. 4:10), and of "in my flesh . . . completing what is lacking [*ta hysterēmata*] in Christ's afflictions for the sake of his body, that is, the church" (Col. 1:24).

Biblical scholars disagree on the literalness with which Paul's language of the church as the body of Christ is to be taken.[8] In contrast to the rhetorical conventions of the ancient Mediterranean world, however, Paul's image of the body functions quite realistically. It affirms that Christ is the source both of the church's identity as a whole and of the identity of each of its members in particular, so that Christ and the church share a common, corporate destiny.

This idea that the church is not just a body in general, but the body of Christ in particular, is reflected in the subsequent development of the metaphor in Colossians and Ephesians, where Christ is spoken of more specifically as the "head" of the body that is the church (Eph. 1:22–23; 5:23; Col. 1:18). While the stimulus for this development of the metaphor must remain a matter of speculation, it has the advantage of making it clear that the church, as the body of Christ, is not a corporate personality in which the particular identity of Jesus is placed on the same level as that of the other members. As the head of the body, Christ is the one "from whom the whole body, nourished and held together by its ligaments and sinews, grows with a growth that is from God" (Col. 2:19; cf. Eph. 4:16). There is thus no possibility that this body's identity will be changed by the addition of new members; it is, rather, the members who are changed by their being "supported" and "held together" under the head.

The characterization of Christ as the head of the church allows further clarification of human beings' status as members of Christ's body. On the one hand, as head, Jesus Christ is the source of the church's

---

8. Thus, while Wayne Meeks downplays the realism of Paul's language of the body on the grounds that his use of the idea "is not materially different from the use by Cicero or Seneca or Plutarch" (Wayne A. Meeks, *The Origins of Christian Morality: The First Two Centuries* [New Haven: Yale University Press, 1993], 134), E. P. Sanders defends "the realism of Paul's view" (E. P. Sanders, *Paul and Palestinian Judaism: A Comparison of Patterns of Religion* [London: SCM, 1977], 522–23).

identity, and thus of the identity of each of the church's members. To use Emmanuel Levinas's language, he is the locus of the church's "face," and thus the one through whom our own status as persons with a "face" is mediated.[9] On the other hand, however, the particularity of Jesus Christ does not exhaust the church's identity. If Christ is the head of the body—so that it is properly called *Christ's* body—he is not himself the whole body. Though our identity as persons before God derives from our life in and under him as the head, our individual stories are also part of his identity as a body, and thus integral to the account that he will give of himself before God on the last day (Matt. 10:32; cf. Luke 12:8).[10] In this context, Jesus' assertion "as you did it to one of the least of these...you did it to me" (Matt. 25:40) should be understood as a corollary to his identity as the Christ and not simply as a metaphorical expression of his love for the vulnerable.

If our status as persons is a function of our incorporation into Christ's body, it might seem to follow that only Christians are persons. Thomas Aquinas addresses this point in the third part of his *Summa Theologiae*, where he devotes considerable attention to Christ's status as head. Citing 1 Tim. 4:10 and 1 John 2:2, Thomas argues that Christ must be understood as the head of Christians and non-Christians alike on the grounds that his headship is the cause rather than the consequence of our salvation (and thus, in the language of the present essay, of our personhood). He then reflects on the different ways in which this headship is realized with respect to particular individuals:

Christ is the head of all human beings, but in different degrees. First and foremost he is the head of those who are united to him in glory; secondly of those who are actually united to him by charity; thirdly, of those who are actually united to him by faith; fourthly, he is the head of those who are only potentially united to him, with a potency that has not yet been activated, although it is to be, according to divine predestination; fifthly,

9. See Emmanuel Levinas, *Totality and Infinity: An Essay on Exteriority* (Pittsburgh: Duquesne University Press, 1969), 194, 197, 203, and passim.

10. "Jesus would not be Christ without his relation to those who are 'in Christ'; he would not be himself" (Francis Watson, *Agape, Eros, Gender: Towards a Pauline Sexual Ethic* [Cambridge: Cambridge University Press, 1999], 140).

he is the head of those who are potentially united to him with a potency that will never be actuated.[11]

Because only those who are incorporated into the body of Christ are saved, ultimately it must be the case that only the elect are persons. Those not acknowledged as persons by the Father or the Son are by definition excluded from life in relationship with God (see Matt. 10:33; Luke 12:9; cf. John 12:48; 1 John 2:19). Because the possibility of such exclusion is reserved to the eschaton, however, it cannot be used as grounds for treating anyone as a nonperson in the present. After all, if Christ is "first and foremost" (*primo et principaliter*) the head only of those united to him in glory, no human being—Christian or not—is fully incorporated into his body (and thus fully realizes her or his identity as a person) in this life; but insofar as Christ functions as Savior precisely in providing expiation for the sins of the whole world (1 John 2:2) irrespective of present confessional status, he is the head of all human beings. It follows that all human beings should be treated as part of his body—and thus as persons—whether or not they appear to be such.

The development that the body metaphor first introduced in Romans and Corinthians undergoes in Colossians and Ephesians suggests that the church is called the body of Christ because Christ is its "head." As head, Christ is the source of the body's unity and thus of its identity. As the one and only human being who is the Word of God incarnate, Jesus is the ground of all human personhood; he alone among human beings is a person in himself. And yet the upshot of the New Testament language of the body of Christ is that the human being Jesus, though a person *in* himself, is not a person *by* himself. In other words, while the *fact* of his personhood is independent of his relationship to other human beings, its *form* is not. On the contrary, because he lives out his personhood as the head of a body that incorporates an indeterminate number of human persons, his identity as a human person is inseparable from his relationship with all these other persons.

This limited degree of mutual definition between Jesus and ourselves means that even though the fact of our personhood is determined exclusively by the relationship Jesus assumes with us, our identity as persons is not simply subsumed by Jesus. Even Paul's famous "I live no longer, but Christ lives in me" (Gal. 2:20) does not

---

11. Aquinas, *Summa Theologiae*, IIIa, q. 8, art. 3; cf. Ia, q. 93, art. 4.

signal a dissolution of individual identity. While there is no room for
setting the individual over against the body in general and the head in
particular (as Paul evidently fears the Corinthians are doing in 1 Cor.
1:10–13), Paul continues to have very clear ideas about the particular
character of his own place within the body (see esp. Galatians 1–2;
cf. Rom. 15:17–24; 1 Cor. 4:14–16). In this way, the fact that there
is but one body does not take away from the plurality of the saints.
Indeed, in a manner analogous to the way in which the communion
of the three persons of the Trinity is the form of divine unity, so the
multiplicity of persons in Christ can be seen as the means by which
God constitutes the body of Christ as one (Eph. 4:11–12).[12]

Once again, in representing us, Jesus does not replace us. Human
beings can be persons because the Word assumed human flesh in Jesus
of Nazareth. That the Word's assumption of human nature takes place
in the life of a particular human being does not compromise its general significance for humankind, because this human life establishes
a repeatable structure for human personhood. This structure, which
is constituted pneumatically as the human being is claimed by God's
Word, is concretized somatically as the persons so claimed are incorporated into Christ's body as members who can neither be replaced
by nor substituted for each other.

THE CHURCH AS ONE AND MANY

Chapter 3 put forward the thesis that our status as persons was bound
up with Christ treating us as such by representing us as persons before
God. This thesis appeared burdened by a basic contradiction, since
any witness comprehensive enough to secure our personhood in the
face of sin and death appeared doomed by that very act to violate
the unrepeatable and inassimilable character of our personhood. Does
the description of the pneumatic and somatic dimensions of human
personhood developed in the preceding sections meet this challenge?

Whether examined in terms of its pneumatic or somatic aspect, it
has been affirmed that Jesus' personhood has an absolute ontological
priority with respect to our own. All human beings, including Jesus, are

---

12. See chapter 8 for further discussion of the relationship between the unity of
humankind and the diversity of human persons.

persons by virtue of their having been claimed by the Word. Having been claimed as persons, they require the gift of the Spirit to live a life that corresponds to this claim. In this sense, all human beings called to be persons form one body, and the fact that Jesus' pneumatically shaped identity is that of the Word establishes him as the head who both directs and represents this body.

Yet Jesus' priority with respect to the rest of the members does not amount to their displacement. Not only is the head not the whole body, but also the body is not a body without the presence of the other members under the head. Far from taking our places, it is in his capacity as the head that Jesus provides the structure within which it makes sense to speak of us having a place at all. To return to the dilemma posed by Ivan Karamazov, Jesus' intercession for the torturer (and, by implication, for the rest of us) does not violate the integrity either of the torturer himself or his victim, because his identity as the head is inseparable from theirs as members of his body.

Importantly, this ability to speak on behalf of others without denying their integrity is proper to the head alone. The victim's mother cannot forgive the torturer on her own account (as Ivan rightly notes), because she, like him, is only the object of God's claiming us as persons in the Word. Jesus alone, as the Word made flesh, is both object and subject of this address and thus the source of the identity of all the members. Yet, for this reason, the mother who has no right to forgive her son's murderer on her own is able to do so in Jesus' name. She herself cannot give the kind of comprehensive witness to the personhood of the torturer that is the necessary condition of affirming him as a person in spite of his crimes; only God can speak the Word that establishes another as a person. But the fact that God has spoken this Word in Jesus means that this witness has been given, and that the mother in Ivan's story can therefore appeal to this objective fact as trumping her own inadequacy no less than the torturer's. In this way, the supremacy of the head, far from undermining the integrity of the members, joins them together in a way that makes possible the kind of relationship between them upon which their life together as one body depends.

It is on the basis of this unity in Christ that it is possible to speak of the church as a collective person. As Hans Urs von Balthasar has argued, such a formulation is dangerous, because it threatens to blur

the distinction between Christ and the church.[13] Nevertheless, the
fact that Jesus is the one in and through whom we are addressed as
persons gives the church a unity that justifies Dietrich Bonhoeffer's
claim that God's call "comes not to the individual, but to the collective person."[14] Bonhoeffer, too, is careful to note that this corporate
address does not obliterate the distinctiveness of the persons who form
the body, since the concrete acts of faith, repentance, judgment, and
grace that this collective address elicits "can only happen 'in' individuals"; nevertheless, "it is not individuals, but the whole community
that, in the individuals, hears, repents, and believes."[15] Within this
conceptual framework our status as individual persons is logically dependent on our identity as a collective person (i.e., as members of the
one body of Christ).[16] Though we are called to be persons as individuals, we are addressed as individuals through Christ who, as the head
of the body, is the immediate object of God's address.

By coming among human beings, Christ transforms their situation
by at once disclosing and effecting their life as one body under himself
as the head. As a divine person, Christ establishes the collective person of the church by claiming particular human persons for his own. In
this way, Christ represents each individual human being before God,
not by taking her or his place, but by giving every human being a
place in his body. Indeed, inasmuch as representation might be taken
to imply absence, Bonhoeffer goes so far as to deny that representation is the best way to characterize Christ's work. As he puts it, "Only
what is not present can be represented. In God's eyes, however, the
church is present in Christ."[17]

In making us part of one body, Christ also changes the significance of our individual bodies. Though our embodiedness is part of
our created nature and therefore "very good" in itself, in the after-
math of the fall our bodies become a manifestation of our alienation
from each other—a source of shame that needs to be covered up

---

13. Von Balthasar, *Persons in Christ,* 342.
14. Dietrich Bonhoeffer, *Sanctorum Communio: A Theological Study of the Sociology of
the Church,* vol. 1 of *Dietrich Bonhoeffer Works,* ed. Clifford J. Green (Minneapolis: Fortress,
1996), 118; cf. 192–208.
15. Ibid., 119.
16. Ibid., 164–65: "the individual is always meant and elected only as a member of the
church-community."
17. Ibid., 157.

(Gen. 3:7). Even though our bodies are connected to one another both through the process of birth and in sexual union (Gen. 2:24; cf. 1 Cor. 6:16), they are experienced as a source of separation. We are all one in Adam, but, as Bonhoeffer notes, this oneness is fragmented—a solidarity in separation from one another and alienation from God.[18] Our bodies identify us as divided from one another as man or woman, Jew or Gentile, slave or free. By taking a body, however, God creates the possibility of overcoming these divisions. It is not that bodily difference is eliminated, or that we cease to be embodied (on the contrary, see Rom. 8:23; cf. 1 Corinthians 15), but that Christ creates a new body in which all our many bodies may find a place.

Because we receive this gift in and through our bodies, this integration is not a fusion but an incorporation. In being made part of the body of Christ, we do not cease to have our own bodies, for it is precisely as the embodied beings we are that Jesus claims us as persons in the first place. But because our lives now have a common referent in Christ, it is both possible and necessary to speak of our many bodies being one body in him. It is on this basis that Christ can be described as the one who "has broken down the dividing wall" of hostility between us, "that he might create in himself one new humanity in place of the two, thus making peace, and might reconcile both groups to God in one body" (Eph. 2:14–16). As the head of every human being, Christ can represent every human person, because every human person is present in him.

And yet if our relationship to God has been made secure in Christ, our relationship to each other requires further clarification. If God sees us in Christ, then our relationship with Christ seems to be the only interpersonal relationship in which we participate that has any real significance for our personhood; and if that is true, then it is hard to know what to make of our diversity as different members of one body. Alternatively, if irreducible distinctiveness is a defining feature of our life as persons in Christ, then how do we in our diversity recognize each other as members of the same body, and not as so many threats to our own relationship to Christ? The next three chapters attempt to address these issues by exploring what the christological matrix of one's own personhood implies about the possibility of encountering others as persons.

---

18. Ibid., 121.

- 5 -

Encountering Others through Jesus Christ

With a degree of consensus verging on unanimity, experts in disciplines ranging from the social sciences to various forms of critical theory argue for the social construction of the human person over against the model of the self-constituting, autonomous individual. The references to poststructuralist analysis of language in chapter 2 echoed this point by showing how our understanding of personhood is shaped from the outset by the inertia of established practices of which we may be only vaguely conscious. In light of the broad weight of opinion in favor of the social construction of personhood, the claim that our status as persons is determined exclusively by the relationship God establishes with us in Jesus Christ can only seem naïve. This chapter will begin to address this challenge by reflecting on the implications of the trinitarian model of personhood presented in the last two chapters for understanding how our relationships with other human beings shape our lives as persons.

The central claim of this model has been that the theological use of the term "person" is rooted in the doctrine of the Trinity, and that its application to human beings must therefore by justified in trinitarian terms. Working within this specifically theological framework, human beings can be called persons only to the extent that they share in the personal life of the triune God. Such sharing is made possible through one of the divine persons having lived a human life as Jesus of Nazareth, thereby both disclosing the personal character of God's own life and opening that life to creaturely participation.

The previous chapter attempted to describe this participation concretely as a process in which God constitutes human beings as persons by addressing them through the same divine Word that is God's own immanent form of self-expression. The most immediate object of this address is Jesus, who is the human form of the Word's address to humankind and thus is himself the Word. Though this model establishes Jesus as the central reference point for every human being's life as a person, it does not, however, necessarily obscure the distinctiveness of other human persons before God. On the contrary, the case was made that it is precisely Jesus' identity as "head" of the body that secures each of us a place as a distinct and irreplaceable "member."

It remains the case, however, that this way of speaking can make our existence as persons seem disturbingly impersonal. To refer to ourselves as "members" of a body ordered under Christ as "head" seems to evacuate our relationships with one another of significance for our identity as persons. Especially in light of the claim that the interpersonal relations that shape the life of the Trinity take the form of mutual commitment, to portray human personhood solely in terms of the individual's relation to Christ would appear no less inconsistent with a strictly trinitarian conception of the person than with various nontheological accounts of human personhood. In light of this latter point in particular, it is necessary to ask whether focus on Jesus as the source and measure of our personhood leaves any place for seeing our relationships with each other as a significant dimension of our lives as persons.

RELATIONAL VIEWS OF PERSONHOOD

The tendency to focus on the structure of relationships between human beings as constitutive of what it means to be a person finds its first clear articulation in the work of Ludwig Feuerbach. Feuerbach formulated his position in explicit opposition to christocentric anthropologies, which, he maintained, effectively undermined the integrity of the mass of human beings by teaching that the fullness of human existence both could be and was in fact realized in one individual considered in isolation from other human beings.[1] In this way, Feuerbach argued, Christianity was untrue to its own affirmations regarding the

---

1. "Here [in Christianity] is entirely wanting the objective perception...that the *thou* belongs to the perfection of the *I*, that *men* are required to constitute humanity, that only men taken together constitute what man should and can be" (Ludwig Feuerbach, *The Essence of Christianity* [New York: Harper, 1957], 155).

central significance of love in human life, since love testifies to the necessary incompleteness of every individual and her fulfillment as a person in relation with others whose difference from herself completes what she lacks. According to Feuerbach, if the perfection of the species were realized in a single individual, "the existence of many [human beings] would be a pure superfluity; a single [human being] would have achieved the ends of the species."[2]

In short, while Feuerbach also had what might be described as a corporate sense of human personhood, he denied that the "body" either did or could have any clearly defined "head." Over against what he perceived as the effective dissolution of concrete individuals in Christ, Feuerbach insisted that the individual human being became a personal "I" only through encountering another human being as an equally personal "Thou."[3] To be person was to be dependent on other persons, and Jesus could not be excepted from this rule without casting doubt on his own personal status.

Though Feuerbach's work was in certain respects foundational, probably no attempt to affirm the relational character of human personhood has been more influential than Martin Buber's.[4] In defining the relationship between persons as fundamental to their constitution as persons, Buber insisted on the integrity of the other as a Thou in the face of every temptation to subject her or him to the self as an "It." Nor was this honoring of the other interpreted by Buber as a matter of charity from which the I might just as easily abstain; on the contrary, since it is only in addressing the Thou that the self acquires its identity as an I, one's own integrity as a person is bound up with acknowledging the other as a Thou. Apart from this pattern of mutual acknowledgement, human beings lose their identity as persons and dissolve into a mass of interchangeable (and thus finally indistinguishable) objects.

In the latter half of the twentieth century, Emmanuel Levinas attempted to deepen Buber's relational model of the person by placing greater emphasis on the concrete particularity of the Thou. In Levinas's view, though Buber rightly stressed that the self only becomes an I in addressing a Thou, he conceived the I-Thou relationship

2. Ibid., 157.
3. Ibid., 158.
4. See Martin Buber, *I and Thou* (Edinburgh: Clark, 1937).

in a purely formal manner that did not recognize the constitutive significance for the I of the Thou's concrete and unsubstitutable particularity. As a result, the Thou appears as little more than the I's external correlate, and thus a creation of the I whose distinctiveness is of no essential concern to the I.[5]

Against this position, Levinas ascribes to the Thou a more determinative role that emphasizes her or his particularity as decisive for the identity of the I. From this perspective, the I or self is characterized by a fundamental passivity that is antecedent to any intentional encounter with the world, and that has as its basic determination the fact of being open to question by the Thou. The self is constituted as a self in this experience of being summoned to respond to a particular other, with the result that the selfhood of the self consists in its responsibility for the other.

In short, for Levinas, the Thou is not primarily the one whom I address, but the one who addresses me, "and in so doing recalls my responsibility, and calls me into question."[6] The self-sufficiency of the ego is thereby undermined at its root, since the I's primordial state of responsibility for the other precedes every possibility of command and control.[7] In this way, Levinas at once challenges and intensifies the idea that encounter with the other is the source of personhood by arguing, in effect, that the presence of the other defines my personhood by calling it into question. It follows that my status as a person is not something that can be established by reference to any capacity of my own, but is from the beginning referred to the fate of the other.

Like Buber (and in distinction from Feuerbach), Levinas does not present his analysis of the self as a rejection of religious accounts of the person. On the contrary, he understands the primordially passive state of the self as rooted in the doctrine of creation, since the logic of being called into existence implies that response to God's summons is necessarily prior to the self-consciousness that would permit either the hearing of or reflection on that summons:

5. See Emmanuel Levinas, "Martin Buber and the Theory of Knowledge," in *The Levinas Reader*, ed. Seán Hand (Oxford: Basil Blackwell, 1989), 72; see also idem, *Totality and Infinity: An Essay on Exteriority* (Pittsburgh: Duquesne University Press, 1969), 68. Cf., for example, Buber, *I and Thou*, 144–47.

6. Levinas, "Ethics as First Philosophy," in *The Levinas Reader*, 83.

7. "Responsibility for another is not an accident that happens to a subject, but precedes essence in it" (Levinas, "Substitution," in *The Levinas Reader*, 104).

In creation, what is called to being answers to a call that could not have reached it since, brought out of nothingness, it obeyed before hearing the order. Thus in the concept of creation *ex nihilo*, if it is not a pure nonsense, there is the concept of a passivity that does not revert into an assumption. The self as a creature is conceived in a passivity more passive still than the passivity of matter, that is, prior to the virtual coinciding of a term with itself.[8]

On the basis of this primordial state of responsibility, Levinas affirms the irreplaceability of each individual. The uniqueness of each self as called into existence is precisely a uniqueness in responsibility, since one's irreplaceability derives from the singularity of one's relationship to the others before whom one is responsible.[9]

Levinas goes on to argue that this primordial state of responsibility for the other is so profound as to constitute what he terms a "substitution," in which I assume the other's place. This substitution does not result in self-alienation, because it derives from the self's own, unique position of responsibility vis-à-vis the other and is thus utterly non-transferable.[10] Neither does it undermine the integrity of the other, since the fundamental condition of substitution is not the freedom of my ego (as though substitution were the product of a personal decision), but responsibility for the other who is already concretely present as one for whom I am responsible prior to any act or attitude that I may assume.[11]

Needless to say, this understanding of substitution is quite different from that to which Sölle objects. The substitution that Sölle critiques is a deliberate act in which Jesus protects my personhood against the threat of dissolution by taking my place. In a manner parallel to Feuerbach, she argues that this way of conceiving human personhood undermines our integrity as persons by rendering our particularity superfluous: the mass of human beings are conceived to be interchangeable selves, with only the life of the substitute retaining distinctive value. By contrast, for Levinas, substitution is not the act

8. Ibid., 103.
9. Ibid., 93.
10. Ibid., 104; cf. 115: "It is as *my own* that substitution for the neighbor is produced."
11. Ibid., 113; cf. 101.

of another on my behalf, but a characteristic of my own existence so fundamental that it is not properly conceived of as an "act" at all. Instead, substitution describes my own life as one confronted with the fact of responsibility for the other. On one level, Levinas's category of substitution refers to the primordial inability of the self to guarantee its own existence. In making use of this category, therefore, Levinas attempts to anchor concrete relationship with the other as deeply as possible in the structure of the self. Relationship is not the expression of selfhood, or even the means by which it is constituted (as in the thought of Feuerbach and Buber), but rather, its essential presupposition. It is only by virtue of the primordial state of my radical responsibility to the other as "substitution" that I have the possibility of personal existence.

THE HUMAN FAILURE TO LIVE IN RELATION

Levinas's insistence on the absolute priority and concrete particularity of the other who establishes the self as a self sets him apart from the more formal accounts of the relationship between I and Thou presented by Feuerbach and Buber. While his emphasis on the unilateral dependence of the self on the other has certain affinities with a christological account of personhood, Levinas shows no interest in identifying the personalizing other exclusively with Jesus of Nazareth. Likewise, while he is considerably more guarded than either Feuerbach or Buber in his assessment of whether the self ever succeeds in practice in acknowledging the structure of responsibility that defines its existence, he falls short of the Christian insistence that the power of sin renders this possibility unrealizable by human effort.[12]

Christians have long seen in the divine declaration that "it is not good that the man should be alone" (Gen. 2:18; cf. vv. 21–24) reason for affirming that human life is characterized by a fundamental orien-

---

12. Levinas argues that one's primordial state of being called into question by the other takes the concrete form of "fear for all the violence and murder my existence might generate, in spite of its conscious and intentional innocence" ("Ethics as First Philosophy," 82). Yet he takes pains to emphasize that this state of radical responsibility is not itself sin, which erupts only when this fear is realized in the self's active pursuit of the other's destruction. See Levinas, "Substitution," 111.

tation to the other. In this respect, the insights of Feuerbach, Buber, and Levinas regarding the relational form of human personhood may be affirmed as fully consistent with the "grammar" of Christian faith. Yet the church's conviction that this primordial orientation is vitiated in practice by the fact of sin makes it necessary to part company with these thinkers when it comes to discussing the form human life together actually takes. Importantly, this parting of the ways is directly connected with the unique role Christians ascribe to Jesus as the one apart from whom the power of sin renders human beings incapable of realizing their created destiny as persons in communion with one another.

The Bible gives no explanation why human beings sin: the fall is portrayed as an inexplicable mystery. What is clear is that sin vitiates the relationships among human beings, and that its effects cannot be undone by human effort. Indeed, when accused by God as a sinner, Adam only compounds the problem by trying to shift the blame to his wife (Gen. 3:12). Within the compass of only a few generations, this attitude of blame turns to murder (Gen. 4:8), and then to a pattern of wholesale slaughter (Gen. 4:23–24), providing graphic illustration of Levinas's insight that the sinful refusal to acknowledge one's responsibility to the other leads inexorably to the destruction of the other.

The catastrophic effects of sin on relationships between human beings, however, must not be allowed to overshadow the fact that in Genesis, sin is in the first instance a violation of humanity's relationship to God. The serpent launches its temptation of the first human pair by suggesting that the God who called them into existence is in fact the enemy of their existence. More specifically, it insinuates that the God who has given human beings a place to dwell is unwilling to make space for them (Gen. 3:1). And while the possibility that rebellion might allow humankind to take God's place is not mooted overtly, it is implicit in the serpent's claim that eating of the tree of knowledge will make Adam and Eve "like God" (Gen. 3:5; cf. v. 22). In this way, human beings' refusal to acknowledge their place under God is depicted as the ground of their failure to acknowledge their responsibility to each other.

As God had warned at the time of creation (Gen. 2:16–17), human beings' violation of the conditions of their creaturely existence under

God only succeeds in undermining that existence. The only way for this threat of nonexistence to be overcome is for the divine other, whose claim human beings have denied, to be heard once again as gracious Sovereign and Creator. Only so can the human self be reestablished in proper creaturely relation both to God and to other people. Yet there are at least two apparently insuperable obstacles to this state of affairs being realized. First, our attempts to hear the other's voice as other are continually vitiated because (as argued in chapter 2) the deliberate attempt to hear an excluded other's voice invariably results in a process of "saming" that assimilates the other's voice to our own. Thus, we continue to be deaf to God's voice, because in a state of sin we find ourselves unable to honor God as genuinely other. Instead (and as observed by Paul in Rom. 1:18–23), we invariably undermine divine otherness by homogenizing God with some aspect of creation.

Though this first obstacle is serious enough, it is rooted in a second one no less profound, which is that our very effort to hear God's voice reflects the presumption that we are capable of securing a place for ourselves before God. This presumption is, of course, false: the only place in which we can stand as human beings is the one we have been allotted by God, and this is just the place we have rejected in rejecting God. Any attempt we may make to return to this place is doomed to fail (Gen. 3:24), since in making such an attempt we presume that our current location—the very place we ought not to be—represents a viable (or at least necessary) starting point for human existence. Thus, all our efforts to get right with God only succeed in confirming our rejection of the one proper option God has allotted us.

Nor can God simply give us a new place without undermining our identity as creatures who were made to occupy the one place we have rejected. Likewise, simply returning us to our original place would compromise our integrity as creatures who have in fact rejected that place. It follows that if we are to be reestablished in our relationship with God (and thereby opened to the possibility of living in relationship with other human beings), it will not be because we come to God, but because God comes to us and makes the place of our destruction—the place where we ought not to be—God's own.

Christians identify Jesus of Nazareth as the one in whom God has done just this. By assuming the conditions of our sinful existence, God takes the place of rejection that we have chosen for ourselves.

Of course, we treat Jesus just as we treat every human other that crosses our path: we attempt to assimilate him, and when that fails, we destroy him. In the case of Jesus, however, the voice of the other is not silenced by death, but proves stronger and more insistent than our capacity for silencing it. That this should be the case is hardly surprising, given that this voice is that of the same Word who called us into existence in the first place, and who is therefore sovereign over the threat of nonexistence. But the fact that the Word confronts us as a human being (and not merely as the transcendent source of human being) represents something genuinely new: in Jesus' resurrection from the dead it turns out that the place of destruction that we had chosen for ourselves—the place that was in itself void of every possibility of genuinely human existence—has been transformed into the place where God chooses to be found. It therefore no longer stands as an obstacle to our living before God and each other as the persons God has elected us to be. Once again, Jesus' work on our behalf, far from displacing us, establishes a place for us in God's life.

THE TRINITARIAN BASIS
OF INTERHUMAN RELATIONS

It needs to be stressed immediately that this possibility is possible only in Jesus. As argued in the previous two chapters, we cannot live before God as persons in our own right. The fact that in his total obedience to God's will Jesus actually succeeded in occupying the place under God that God intended for all human beings means that in Jesus, human personhood is fully and finally realized. It follows that in the final analysis we know that life as a person is characterized by the kind of openness to the other described by Feuerbach, Buber, and Levinas only because that is the kind of life Jesus lived. Insofar as this life reveals Jesus as the divine Word who is both spoken by the Father and who, as such, proclaims the Father's rule, we are led back to the principle that "person" refers properly to the divine hypostases. If human beings can claim to the status of persons, it is only because they are caught up in their life.

Because the status of the Father, Son, and Spirit as persons is not reducible to any common denominator, each may be supposed to live as a person differently.[13] These differences are reflected in the different relations in which they stand one to another. The fact that only one of these persons, the Word, becomes a creature therefore dictates that all creaturely personhood is mediated through the Word, so that we are not persons in the mode of the Father or the Spirit. In other words, if our status as persons is bound up with our sharing in the trinitarian communion of the Godhead, its particular character is defined by the Word as the divine person in whom this sharing takes place.

If we wish to know the way in which the Word is a person, we have no other reference point than the career of Jesus. In broadest terms, this career is bracketed by two complementary events: his being sent by the Father in the incarnation and his being glorified by the Spirit in his resurrection and ascension. Following the principle that God's "economic" actions in history reflect the trinitarian persons' "immanent" relationships in eternity, we can describe the Word's personal existence as having its origin in being spoken *forth* by the Father and its completion in being spoken *back* to the Father by the Spirit. In coming forth from the Father, the Word is the form of divine *self-expression;* in being confessed by the Spirit as the Father's own, the Word is confirmed as *divine* self-expression.

This characterization should not be taken to imply that the Word is a purely passive member of the Trinity, for the Word is also the Son who, in being sent by the Father, both bears witness to the Father's rule and bestows the Father's Spirit on his disciples. Moreover, commitment to Chalcedonian Christology dictates that these activities are performed in Jesus' divine and human natures both. At the same time, however, it is part and parcel of the doctrine of the hypostatic union that Jesus' human nature is passive with respect to determining his status as a person. His personhood is established solely by the fact that his human nature is enhypostasized by the Word.

That human personhood is realized concretely as encounter with an other is therefore based in the divine other having first encountered and claimed us in Jesus. It is only as addressed by this particular "Thou" that a human being is constituted as a person. Nor, once again, should it be supposed that our status as persons depends on our giving

---

13. See Wolfhart Pannenberg, *Systematic Theology*, vol. 1 (Grand Rapids: Eerdmans, 1991), 428.

an adequate response to this address. To be sure, the New Testament leaves little doubt that our life as persons is fulfilled only insofar as the Spirit inspires us to address God as "Father"—and one another as brothers and sisters—in the same way that Jesus does (Rom. 8:15; Gal. 4:6; cf. Matt. 6:9 and par.); but that does not mean that we do not qualify as persons until then. Our qualification rests exclusively in the work of Jesus Christ.

That we may fail to live out the life of communion to which we are called in Jesus is recognized in the tradition as the threat of damnation, or eternal exclusion from God's presence. But until and unless this awful possibility is realized at the last day, *it is the fact that the Word continues to be addressed to us, irrespective of the presence or quality of response on our part, that constitutes us as persons.* Our status as persons is thus divorced from any human capacity, even if our destiny as persons takes the form of the fulfillment of those capacities, through Christ, in communion with God and one another.

THE CONCRETE OTHER
AND THE ETERNAL THOU

To summarize the results of the preceding sections, the Christian tracing of personhood to the action of God in Christ is not meant to suggest that our relationships with other human beings are irrelevant to the content of our lives as persons. Nevertheless (and in line with what was said in chapter 4), the way in which we live out our lives as persons needs to be distinguished from the question of who or what makes us persons in the first place. To live as persons is to live a life oriented to the other, but we are persons by virtue of God's action toward us in Christ quite apart from our assuming any such orientation.

Yet if we are forbidden by the utterly gracious character of our election as persons from correlating the *fact* of any human being's status as a person with either the presence of or even the perceived capacity for explicit response to Jesus, our *perception* of an individual's personhood cannot be separated from its christological ground in the same way. If those around us are constituted as persons by God in Christ whether they know it or not, this very point dictates that they cannot be perceived as persons (in the specifically trinitarian sense of the term) apart from Christ. Because human beings *are* persons only "in" Christ, they cannot be encountered *as* persons apart from Christ. As Bonhoeffer put it, "We can meet others only through the mediation of Christ."[14]

This insistence on the christological mediation of interpersonal relationships can appear unsettlingly indirect (and in this respect impersonal) when compared to the models proposed by Feuerbach, Buber, and Levinas. While all three thinkers recognize a variety of ways in which the encounter between I and Thou can fail, all of them view the possibility of such a direct encounter as an essential feature of human being. Indeed, Buber holds that relationships with other human beings mediate our relationship with God, who, as the "eternal Thou" is perceived and addressed through the particular human other.[15] By contrast, a thoroughly christological account of human personhood allows for no relationship to the human other prior to or apart from one's relationship to God in Jesus Christ.[16] Jesus is not simply a moral example who illustrates how to relate to the other as a Thou (though he is certainly also this), but the Thou who is the condition of the possibility of every such relationship—a situation that appears to bring us back to Feuerbach's objection that positing Christ alone as the model human being undermines the concrete reality of human being realized in relationship with others.

Fortunately, the interpretation of Christ's personhood offered in the previous section contains the resources necessary to answer this charge. As the second person of the Trinity, Jesus is not a person in isolation, but in relation to the Father and the Spirit. Nor is the relational character of his existence limited to the other persons of the Trinity: having become flesh, the Word is also the "son of Mary and the brother of James and Joses and Judas and Simon" (Mark 6:3). To be sure, he is not a person *because of* these latter relationships, but neither is he the person he is *apart from* them. In this respect, Jesus' personhood is isomorphic with our own: though (in line with our insistence that we are persons solely by virtue of God's addressing us as such in Christ) our interhuman relationships do not make us

---

14. Dietrich Bonhoeffer, *Life Together* (New York: Harper & Row, 1954), 36; cf. 32–33.

15. "In each [particular] Thou we address the eternal Thou"; also, "Every particular Thou is a glimpse through to the eternal Thou" (Buber, *I and Thou*, 6, 75).

16. Buber, by contrast, sees Jesus' relationship to the God he calls Father as universalizable (*I and Thou*, 67).

persons, our life *as* persons is nevertheless shaped by the particularity of these relationships.

Here again the unique shape of Jesus' life *as* a person both can and must be distinguished from the reasons why he *is* a person. Only Jesus is himself God's Word made flesh, and this fact gives his life as a person a unique shape; but even this uniqueness has a formal parallel with other human beings, since the peculiar form of our relationships with each other dictates that the shape of every human being's life *as* a person is unique. By contrast, that every human being *is* a person is established prior to and apart from the particular form of life we lead (or fail to lead) *as* persons by God's unilateral decision to claim us in the Word.

In this way, the claim that the status of human beings as persons is determined unilaterally by God in Christ does not undermine the relational form of human personhood. Like all other human beings, Jesus *is* a person only by virtue of his having been claimed by the Word, but the particular shape of his existence *as* a person is insepa-rable from his relationships with other human beings. The claim that other human beings fulfill their identity as persons only insofar as they confess Jesus as Savior reflects the basic conviction that Jesus is the source of our personhood; but it in no sense renders relationships with other human beings irrelevant to the shape of personal existence. In-deed, insofar as Jesus is the one who reestablishes our relationship with God as creatures not destined to be alone, it is precisely our rela-tionship to him that discloses to us the personal significance of other human beings.

Because Jesus' is the life in which all human beings are claimed as persons, it follows that we are able to relate to other human beings as persons only in light of their relationship to Jesus, or, to use more traditional language, only when we see them "in" Christ. Once again, this act of seeing in no way constitutes others as persons; that has been accomplished by God's sending of Jesus prior to and indepen-dently of any reaction on our part or theirs. Nor should it be supposed that we can treat the content of Jesus' identity as fixed over against our encounter with others. On the contrary, in the same way that our experience of other human beings is transformed in light of Christ, so our knowledge of Christ is constantly augmented in light of our expe-rience of those other human beings whom God has claimed as persons in him. In short, while Jesus is the touchstone for our understanding of human personhood, he is not its entire content.

Setting personhood within this christological framework requires a modification of Buber's idea that the "particular Thous" whom we encounter in time and space are a window to the "eternal Thou" of God. This modification is not a simple reversal, as though it were being claimed that we are able to see particular human beings as persons only by way of a disembodied experience of the divine. Rather, the Christian claim is that it is through the particular person Jesus—whose status as "eternal Thou" is revealed in the historical particularity of his life, death, and resurrection—that we encounter other human beings as the persons they have been called to be in him.

Nor should this process of seeing others in Christ be confused with the idea of trying to see the face of Jesus in the other. For one thing (and once again in line with the analysis presented in chapter 2), any ideas we might have of Jesus' face may be expected to be far more creations of our own imaginations—and thus, in the final analysis, images of ourselves—than authentic portraits. But even if it were possible for us to distinguish Christ's face from our own prejudices, projecting that face onto others would only serve to obscure their own distinctive identities as persons. Such a practice is not consistent with the gospel, according to which the presence of Jesus summons us to take the particularity of the other seriously (see, e.g., Matt. 25:31–46). Our task as persons in Christ is thus not to fold the other into Jesus, but rather to allow Jesus to show us the other.

This claim that our encounter with the "eternal Thou" in Jesus Christ is the condition of personal encounter with the "particular Thou" is reflected in Jesus' own teaching. In response to a lawyer's query regarding the relative priority of the commandments, Jesus teaches that "the greatest and first commandment" is to love God; the second (which is "like it") is to love one's neighbor (Matt. 22:36–40 and pars.). The significance of this ordering has been the object of considerable debate,[17] but the line of reasoning in the previous paragraph suggests at the very least caution in concluding that Jesus intends to relegate the neighbor to second place in a way that would

17. Karl Barth, for example, takes pains to note that Jesus' close correlation of these two commandments does not take away from the fact that there remains a genuine distinction between them (CD, III/2, 216–17).

allow for the possibility of a situation in which love of neighbor would be in conflict with love of God. Paul illustrates just how inconceivable such a situation is from a Christian point of view in the opening verses of Romans 9. In asserting that he could wish himself "accursed and cut off from Christ" for the sake of his fellow Jews, not only does he rule out the possibility that love of God could ever be played off against love of neighbor, but he also bears indirect testimony to the fact that the desire to be cut off from Christ for the other's sake is itself a sign of the deepest solidarity with Christ, who himself was cut off (Gal. 3:13) for the sake of the other. Interpreted in this light, Jesus' placing love of God first does not signal the occlusion of the neighbor, but rather, it points to the circumstances in which love of neighbor becomes truly possible.

THE GOOD SAMARITAN
AS A PARABLE OF PERSONHOOD

This point is made especially clear in Luke's account of Jesus' teaching on the great commandment. Here the lawyer does not ask which commandment is the greatest, but rather, what he needs to do to inherit eternal life (Luke 10:25). Under counterquestioning from Jesus, he acknowledges that the requirements are clearly set out in the law as love of God and neighbor (v. 27). The story might well end there (as it does in the Matthean and Markan parallels), but Luke has the lawyer go on to ask Jesus, "And who is my neighbor?" (v. 29). Although we have already had occasion to note that scripture contains no formal discussion of personhood as such, this question seems to be prompted by many of the same concerns that animate modern debates over who qualifies as a person.

The fact that this question is put into the mouth of a lawyer highlights its parallelism with contemporary discussion of personhood, inasmuch as the latter also tend to surface in specifically legal contexts. Because persons are understood to have a right to a certain level or quality of treatment—one that would rule out, for example, their being made the objects of medical experimentation without their prior consent—it is necessary to have some criteria for determining who counts as a person. In other words, insofar as persons constitute a class of beings whom I am not allowed to treat with the same kind of indifference I might a rock or a tree, they confront me with certain obligations and place definite restrictions on my own freedom of action.

When the matter is put in this way, concern over one's own ethical liability has seemingly eclipsed any genuine interest in the well-being of others. It is therefore not surprising that the lawyer in Luke 10—who, we are told, asks his question about the identity of his neighbor out of a wish to "vindicate" or "justify" (*dikaiōsai*) himself—tends to be viewed in a rather unfavorable light. It should be noted, however, that one need not view his question as prompted purely by the selfish desire to avoid censure or minimize personal responsibility. If nothing less than eternal life hangs on my love of neighbor, then it is only natural that I should want to determine just who my neighbor is. From this perspective, the lawyer's question to Jesus is a sign of no greater presumption or recalcitrance than the ethically serious efforts of participants in contemporary debates over abortion and euthanasia to find a coherent definition of the person.

Whatever the lawyer's motives in asking his question, Jesus responds by telling the parable of the good Samaritan. The story's plot is straightforward enough: a man (presumably Jewish, inasmuch as his journey begins in Jerusalem) is assaulted on his way to Jericho and left for dead by the roadside. A priest and a Levite, nervous over the possibility of becoming ritually unclean through contact with a corpse, pass him by. It is a despised Samaritan, evidently unconcerned about any possible effects on his ritual purity,[18] who comes to the victim's aid by tending his wounds, bringing him to a place of shelter, and instructing the innkeeper to spare no expense in his treatment.

Does this story answer the lawyer's question? Considered by itself, the story of the man who fell among thieves might lead the reader (who shares the lawyer's perspective as the one to whom the tale is told) to suppose that the neighbor is the man in need. On this reading, the details of the story are ultimately superfluous, and the parable is only a more or less engaging way of illustrating a fairly straightforward answer to the lawyer's question: your neighbor is anyone who needs your care.

---

18. The Samaritan Pentateuch contained the same injunctions against contact with the dead as the one the priest and the Levite would have consulted.

Yet this is not how Jesus himself makes use of the parable. He ends the tale not with a neatly drawn conclusion (e.g., "Count as your neighbor anyone in need"), but with a question of his own: "Which of these three seems to you to have been a neighbor to the one who fell among thieves?" (v. 36). If the parable appears at first glance to accept the terms of the lawyer's question (i.e., the problem of identifying who counts as a neighbor), Jesus' counterquestion redirects attention from the status of others to that of the lawyer himself. As it turns out, "neighbor" is not a category that the lawyer is authorized to apply to others; instead, it takes the form of a challenge and recoils back upon him as a moral agent capable either of being or of failing to be a neighbor to someone else.[19] In this way, Jesus asks lawyer and reader alike to consider the possibility that the question of our own status as neighbors (and, by extension, as "persons") might be anthropologically prior to any reflection on the status of other people.

Jesus does not so much answer the lawyer's question as turn it around. His counterquestion forces the lawyer to apply the term "neighbor" not to the victim of the assault, but to "the one who showed [literally, 'did'] compassion to him" (Luke 10:37). This is not to suggest that the effect of Jesus' question is merely to replace one possible definition of the neighbor ("someone in need") with another ("one who meets others' needs"). Indeed, it would be hard to imagine a more serious misinterpretation of the parable than the conclusion that the neighbor is the class of those who show mercy to the afflicted— as though one would be justified in refusing to classify as a neighbor anyone who fails to show mercy in the way the Samaritan did.

Rather, the crucial feature of the parable is that Jesus refrains from offering *any* definition of the neighbor.[20] It is true that the one who showed compassion was a neighbor to the man who fell among thieves, but Jesus' final words to the lawyer are in the imperative rather than the indicative mood: "Go and do likewise." The lawyer is not told who

---

19. See J. M. Creed, *The Gospel according to St. Luke: The Greek Text, with Introduction, Notes, and Indices* (London: Macmillan, 1930), 151.

20. Joseph Fitzmyer is thus right to conclude, "No definition of 'neighbor' emerges from the 'example,' because such a casuistic question is really out of place." His judgment here, however, conflicts rather sharply with his earlier statement (on the same page!): "The point of the story is . . . that a 'neighbor' is anyone in need with whom one comes into contact and to whom one can show pity and kindness" (*The Gospel according to Luke: Introduction, Translation, and Notes*, vol. 2 [New York: Doubleday, 1985], 884).

his neighbor is. He is simply commanded to imitate the Samaritan's compassion without being given any specific criteria regarding those to whom compassion is owed.

Admittedly, this reading of the parable does not seem especially useful for resolving those contemporary ethical dilemmas in which the question of personhood figures prominently. To all appearances, it amounts to a conceptually vacuous latitudinarianism in which I am obliged to consider every needy being I encounter as a person. Yet it is precisely in the face of such concerns that the story of the good Samaritan can serve as steadying theological ballast. To be sure, an important feature of that parable is Jesus' refusal to satisfy the lawyer's desire for a readily applicable anthropology. The neighbor is defined neither as the one in need nor as the one who shows compassion to the needy. But by effectively invalidating the lawyer's question, Jesus asks the reader to consider that the crucial anthropological issue is not the status of the other whom I face, but rather, who I am.

In working out the implications of this latter point, it is worth recalling that throughout most of the church's history the parable of the good Samaritan has been interpreted christologically. According to this reading, the man who falls among thieves represents humankind, half-dead from its sins; the Samaritan is Jesus, who brings us back to life as the persons we were created to be. If the foregoing analysis of the parable is at all accurate, this traditional interpretation may not be as far-fetched as the majority of twentieth-century interpreters suppose.[21] As already noted, the lawyer's question assumes that the status of the other is the theological problem. He takes his own status as a person for granted and sees the other as the one whose status is open to question: love is something he is obliged to show the other— if the other qualifies as a neighbor. But Jesus' counterquestion turns things around: the neighbor in the story is not the one in need of our love (as the lawyer's question implied) but the one who loves us.[22]

In this way, the logic of the parable redirects the question of who

---

21. Not that modern attempts to affirm a christological interpretation of the parable have been altogether lacking. See, for example, Jean Daniélou, "Le bon Samaritain," in *Mélanges bibliques rédigés en l'honneur de Andree Robert* (Paris: Bloud et Gay, 1957), 457–65, and B. Gerhardsson, *The Good Samaritan—The Good Shepherd?* (Lund: Gleerup, 1958).

22. "For the question 'Which one was neighbour to the man who was waylaid?' requires that the answer be given from the position of the man in trouble; that the lawyer put himself in the place of the waylaid man" (L. P. Trudinger, "Once Again, Now 'Who Is

qualifies as a person from the other to the self. By implicitly calling the listener's status into question, the parable casts us in the role of the half-dead victim, with the implication that we first need to be shown compassion by a neighbor as a condition of becoming neighbors ourselves (cf. Eph. 4:32). If "neighbor" in the parable is the functional equivalent of "person," it follows that our status as persons can no more be taken for granted than the recovery of the man set upon by thieves. Rather, this status requires a prior act of compassion in which another person treats us as a person. If we adhere both to a trinitarian framework in our use of the term "person" and to the conviction that only one of those persons has become flesh and dwelt among us, no human being but Jesus can assume the role of the Samaritan for us.

Nor is a christological exegesis of the parable lacking in resources for ethical reflection. An unspoken assumption underlying the lawyer's original question to Jesus is that once the identity of my neighbor has been ascertained, the course of action that follows is clear. In other words, the lawyer seems to have no doubts about what love of neighbor entails, only about the range of its application. The same set of assumptions seems to underlie much of the contemporary quest for a criteriology of personhood. Thus, if the fetus is a person, then I should not abort it; if my comatose aunt is a person, I should not withdraw life support; if monkeys have a claim to personhood, I should not subject them to medical experiments.

Upon further reflection, however, the idea that the range of beings to whom love is to be shown is more problematic than the content of the love itself seems a rather odd assumption. Is the status of the other as a person really that crucial to our moral reasoning? After all, though I am quite confident that my wife (for example) is a person, that confidence certainly does not by itself provide me with clear guidelines about how I should behave toward her in any given situation. Indeed, it is precisely in my marriage—arguably the most "personal" relationship I have with another human being (at least as compared with my more formal and routinized relations with the mail carrier, the checkout clerk, or even my colleagues at work)—that I find myself most regularly having to ask myself what love requires.

My Neighbour?'" *Evangelical Quarterly* 48 [1976]: 161). Cf. Robert W. Funk, "The Good Samaritan as Metaphor," *Semeia* 2 (1974): 79.

This is not to deny all moral relevance to reflection on the status of the other. If my wife were to become critically ill and unable to make decisions regarding her own care, my understanding of her condition and prognosis would certainly contribute to any decisions I might be asked to make on her behalf. I suspect, however, that my thinking would not turn on the question of whether or not she still qualified as a person. The parable of the good Samaritan provides good theological basis for this suspicion, insofar as this story suggests that the more important ethical question is not whether my wife is a person, but rather how I, as one who has been treated as a person by Jesus Christ, should relate to my wife (or anyone else) as the person I have been called to be. In other words, the crucial ethical judgment in my behavior toward those I meet on the road is not primarily the determination of the general category under which they fall (however unavoidable some such judgment may be), but rather, the way in which I define my relationship to them in their particularity.[23]

This way of addressing the question of personhood requires a profound shift from the presuppositions underlying most analyses of what it means to be a person. Instead of making my own personhood the implicit presupposition for evaluating that of others, the story of the good Samaritan calls my own status as a person into question. This process takes different forms according to one's place with respect to the powers that define what it is to be a person in a given context. For those who have traditionally been excluded from consideration as persons, questioning of their status will mean license "to engage in a political and theoretical process of constituting themselves as subjects of knowledge and history."[24] For those whose status as persons has been taken for granted, the same practice will demand a conscious rejection of their normative status. In both cases, the reference point for practice will be encounter with the neighbor, understood as the one whose identity is not given in advance.

---

23. See Stanley Hauerwas, "Must a Patient Be a Person to Be a Patient? Or, My Uncle Charlie Is Not Much of a Person but He Is Still My Uncle Charlie," in *Truthfulness and Tragedy: Further Investigations in Christian Ethics* (Notre Dame, Ind.: Notre Dame University Press, 1977), 130.

24. Elisabeth Schüssler Fiorenza, *Rhetoric and Ethic: The Politics of Biblical Studies* (Minneapolis: Fortress, 1999), 46. Schüssler Fiorenza denies that this process is christologically mediated, however; indeed, she argues that "focusing on the figure of Christ, the Lord and Son of the Father, doubles wo/men's self-alienation" (p. 94).

Jesus is the primary instance of the neighbor whose identity is not given, because Jesus is the one who calls us to the road of discipleship. But nothing could be further from the truth than to conclude that our task is therefore to seek out people who look like Jesus. As the many "quests for the historical Jesus" have shown, to pursue that aim only succeeds in reintroducing us to ourselves in a way that simply confirms our existing beliefs and prejudices. In line with the preliminary conclusions reached at the end of chapter 2, it therefore seems better to conceive Jesus' work as teaching us that the neighbor is other than him in the same way that he is other than us.

At this point, however, we are confronted with a still more serious problem. The thesis that we encounter the other as a person only through Jesus—and, with it, the idea that Jesus refers us to others as persons—presupposes that we do in fact encounter Jesus in time and space. Yet it is a fact accepted by Christians no less than by nonbelievers that Jesus has not walked the earth for nearly two millennia. This absence would appear to make encountering him impossible, and thereby undermine the claim that we encounter others through him. The crucial position ascribed to Jesus in mediating our relationships to other persons therefore demands some account of his continued presence. The next chapter attempts to provide such an account.

- 6 -

Encountering Jesus Christ in Others

In the previous chapter I tried to give greater depth to the claim that Jesus checks the occlusion of the other by exploring how the relationship that Jesus establishes with us affects our relationships with each other. It was not my intent to suggest that reference to Jesus magically suspends the play of differences on which our language for talking about persons (or anything else) depends. Within the church no less than outside of it, such talk will continue to be marked by the trace of the neighbor whose difference is suppressed through homogenization or occlusion. My claim was simply that attention to the particularity of Jesus has the capacity to disrupt the smooth functioning of such occlusion.

It should not be supposed that this capacity is realized automatically through the mere fact of Christian confession. After all, Christians paint pictures of Jesus that correspond to their own limited visions of humanity all the time. The Spanish conquistadors had one vision of Jesus, nineteenth-century liberals another; and in hindsight the degree to which both groups constructed Jesus in their own image is painfully clear. The words of which the biblical story of Jesus are composed have no magical ability to block this process, and no theology should suggest otherwise. It is not the words we use to describe Jesus, but Jesus himself who disrupts our views of the person by showing the neighbor to us. To be sure, Christians proceed on the basis of their experience that the biblical words that tell the Jesus story (or, more accurately, the preaching of these words) function as the means through which Jesus encounters and claims us; but the initiative remains always and exclusively with Jesus.

This affirmation of Jesus' freedom of action now brings us to the

83

question with which the last chapter ended: How can one who is confessed as exalted to God's right hand continue to be present with us in time and space? This problem famously underlies the differing understandings of the eucharist that divided the Reformation in the sixteenth century, with the Lutherans maintaining that Christ's presence in the consecrated elements did not compromise confession of his exalted status, and the Reformed insisting that taking Christ's session at God's right hand seriously meant denying his physical presence in the world. Even if the divergent views adopted at that time are no longer judged church dividing, the sacramental focus of the controversy reflects two basic dimensions of Christ's continuing presence in the world: the Holy Spirit and the church. While these two are by no means mutually exclusive or, indeed, even patient of coherent articulation independently of one another, they are distinct enough to merit separate treatment.

CHRIST'S PRESENCE IN THE HOLY SPIRIT AND THE SACRAMENTS

In his subtle and carefully argued book, *The Identity of Jesus Christ,* Hans Frei defends the proposition that grasping Jesus' identity as narrated in the Gospels is inseparable from acknowledging his ongoing presence as risen Savior. According to Frei, to understand who the Jesus of the Gospels is, is to acknowledge him as risen and, therefore, present.[1] While the claim that he is risen and ascended to the right hand of God means that he is not present to us now in the way he was in the years 1–30, this transcendence of the limits of his earthly lifespan is a function of his identity as the man born of Mary and crucified under Pilate. In short, the particular shape of Jesus' identity is such that though he lived in the past, he is not restricted to it.[2]

This argument suggests that Christian interpretations of Jesus ought to be characterized by modesty and sobriety, since they remain subject to correction by Jesus himself as risen Savior. And yet Jesus can challenge us only if he is present to us, and such presence seems impossible in light of his own particularity as the one who has ascended to the

---

1. Hans W. Frei, *The Identity of Jesus Christ: The Hermeneutical Bases of Dogmatic Theology* (Eugene, Oreg.: Wipf and Stock, 1997), 179.
2. See Barth's discussion of Jesus as Lord of time in *CD* III/2, esp. 474–78.

right hand of God. Frei gives an excellent account of the difficulty of talking coherently about "presence" in such circumstances. What we have, he writes,

> is not [Christ's] own self-focused presence, but a diffused presence that seems strangely elusive and haunting as well as difficult to describe: It is that of ourselves, individually or collectively, seeking to grasp identity from the fear of nonidentity, presence in the midst of the fact and conviction of fleetingness.[3]

In short, if we continue to know Christ as risen Savior, we no longer know him according to the flesh (2 Cor. 5:16). But how, then, can we be said to know him at all, if we are not simply to be thrown back on the raw data of the biblical narratives, with all our potential for twisting them according to our own prejudices?

One way that Christians answer this question is to say that Christ is known in the Holy Spirit. As noted earlier, the evangelists all agree in assigning the Holy Spirit a central role in defining Jesus' identity: it was through the Spirit that Jesus was conceived, commissioned for his public ministry, sustained in that ministry, and, finally, raised from the dead.[4] After Jesus' ascension, however, the Spirit is evidently decoupled from him in a way that permits its general outpouring on his disciples (John 7:39; 16:7; cf. Luke 24:49; Acts 1:8; 2:33). In this way, the sending of the Spirit is for the writers of the New Testament correlated with Jesus' absence (Luke 24:46–49; John 14:16–17; 16:7; cf. Matt. 10:20 and pars.). Yet this correlation in no way diminishes the Spirit's christological orientation: the Spirit's role is to teach people about Jesus (Luke 12:2; John 15:26–27; 1 Cor. 2:13), and the relationship between them is so close that it is possible to call the Spirit the Spirit of Jesus (Acts 16:6–7; 1 Pet. 1:11), and even to say that Jesus is the Spirit (2 Cor. 3:17–18; cf. 1 Cor. 15:45).

As closely identified as the Spirit and Jesus may be, however, Jesus' presence in the Spirit is not the same as it was prior to Good Friday, or even during the forty days after Easter. As Frei notes, to say that Jesus is present in the Spirit is to affirm that his presence is indirect.[5] This indirectness follows from the confession that Jesus' resurrected

---

3. Frei, *Identity of Jesus Christ,* 186.
4. See p. 52.
5. Frei, *Identity of Jesus Christ,* 187.

body, while retaining its particularity, is no longer in the realm of space and time, so that presence cannot be interpreted in terms of spatial or local proximity.[6] This does not mean that Jesus' presence in the Spirit is to be understood as a thought or a feeling inside us. If it were, then its objectivity would be lost. On the other hand, neither can his presence be interpreted as a matter of continuity in space, both because Jesus' body is ascended outside of the spatiotemporal realm, and because it is precisely the Spirit's freedom from these temporal and spatial constraints that is the source of its power to challenge our views of who Jesus is.[7]

This image of a presence that is both free from spatiotemporal constraints and fully objective is consistent with the Johannine image of a Spirit whose freedom as a power that "blows where it chooses" (such that "you do not know where it comes from or where it goes") remains concrete enough that "you hear the sound of it" (John 3:8). We cannot establish a chain of events that brings Jesus' Spirit to a particular place in the same way that we could, for example, explain Jesus' presence in Jerusalem at Passover by reference to a journey from Galilee that is in principle physically traceable. Nevertheless, the Spirit's presence is verifiable by its confession of Jesus as the Lord (1 Cor. 12:3) who has come in the flesh (1 John 4:2). In this way, the New Testament authors make it clear that the Spirit encounters us from without, in particular words and (to the extent that words acquire their meaning only within the practices that shape the wider cultural-linguistic context) deeds.

Yet this conclusion still leaves open the question of exactly how the Spirit confronts us. Unlike the Trinity's second person, the Spirit is not incarnate (again, an inability to be pinned down is one of the Spirit's chief characteristics); nor does the Spirit's voice sound from heaven in the manner that the Father's does at Jesus' baptism (Matt. 3:17 and pars.) and Transfiguration (Matt. 17:5 and pars.; cf. John 12:28). Instead, the Spirit's speech is mediated through the words and actions

---

6. "God has and knows various modes of being at a given place, and not only the single mode which the philosophers call local or spatial" ("Formula of Concord," Epitome, art. 7, in *The Book of Concord: The Confessions of the Evangelical Lutheran Church*, ed. Theodore G. Tappert [Philadelphia: Muhlenberg, 1959], 483).

7. As Frei puts it, Christ's presence "must have a spatial and temporal basis without itself being subject to these confinements in such a way as to be trammeled in its freedom" (*Identity of Jesus Christ*, 187).

of human beings: we hear the Spirit—and thus encounter Jesus—in the voices of our neighbors' testimony to Jesus as the risen one. In this respect, the claim that Jesus' presence among us in the Spirit is indirect does not mean that it is disembodied.[8] If, as argued in the last chapter, we are able to meet the neighbor as a person only in Jesus, it must now be added that we meet Jesus only in the neighbor. Though the Spirit is not incarnate, it nevertheless works through the flesh-and-blood existence of human beings who are the vehicles of the Spirit's testimony. This does not entail any weakening of the principle that we can see other human beings as persons only through Jesus; for if we encounter Jesus only through the Spirit-inspired witness of our neighbor, that witness stands between us and our neighbor as that which confronts us with the presence of Jesus and *thereby* of the human person who testifies to him.

Because the Spirit blows where it wills, the presence of Christ is not subject to manipulation or control, but that does not make it simply random. The witness in and through which the Spirit is active takes concrete form in the church's twofold proclamation of word and sacrament. Though these two have as their content nothing other than the Jesus whose life is the subject of the biblical texts, their public and external character are integral to their mediation of the presence of the risen one. In this context, Luther's insistence that the gospel is properly spoken rather than written can be understood as a reminder that what is fixed in writing can all too easily be interpreted as a datum under my control.[9] When this happens, the life of Jesus ceases to be Jesus' life and becomes merely a shadow of my own, with the result that I am insulated both from the disorienting shock of experiencing Jesus' presence and call, and from the grace that comes in and through this shock. My own thoughts about Jesus, however biblically informed they may be, do not amount to an encounter with Jesus. Precisely because Jesus is present only in the Spirit, we cannot

---

8. "[A] disembodied person, a 'Jesus' whose presence was a merely 'spiritual' presence in our 'inner' selves, would be...no person at all....If the Lord is present as the speaking of the gospel, his presence is...embodied" (Eric W. Gritsch and Robert W. Jenson, *Lutheranism: The Theological Movement and Its Confessional Writings* [Philadelphia: Fortress, 1976], 86).

9. Martin Luther, "A Brief Instruction on What to Look for and Expect in the Gospels," in *Word and Sacrament I*, vol. 35 of *Luther's Works*, ed. E. Theodore Bachmann (Philadelphia: Fortress, 1960), 123.

presume to come to Jesus; rather, we must trust that Jesus comes to us through word and sacrament.

All this is simply to reiterate that we are persons only insofar as God addresses us, and that this address, because it is from God, necessarily comes upon us from without. What is added here is that it comes to us indirectly, as the Spirit of Christ encounters us through the humanly mediated forms of word and sacrament. In this encounter the neighbor is not simply a conduit whose own personal presence can be ignored. Because we are persons only as we have been addressed by a person, we cannot take this address seriously unless we regard the one through whom it comes to us as herself a person. To be sure, in the word that is spoken I encounter Jesus before my neighbor, but in the moment that I find myself addressed by Jesus through the neighbor, I am compelled to recognize her personhood as a condition of my own.

Nor does the personhood of my neighbor cease to be a condition of my own when roles are reversed, and I serve as the witness through whom Christ confronts her. I certainly cannot view personhood as a quality that I am free to bestow on or withhold from her, because it is not a quality that I possess in my own right. Because I can only address my neighbor as a person in the same Spirit through whom I have been so addressed, my decision to do so is not subject to my own discretion. Though I remain responsible for my behavior when I address my neighbor as a person, in addressing her I am simply confirming a claim on her that God has already made apart from me. If I fail to confirm the Word that God has already spoken by withholding my address, I deny my own personhood no less than hers, since my life as a person in Christ takes concrete form in addressing other members of his body as persons. Where I fail to do this, I have failed to see Christ as the head who claims my neighbor no less than myself, and thus have undermined my own status as a member of his body. The indirectness of Christ's presence in the word thus means that I cannot view my own personhood independently of my neighbor's, whether I am considered as the means or the object of the Spirit's address.

The same indirect presence of Christ in the Spirit underlies the sacraments, which are in this respect quite properly characterized as "visible words." The sacraments' visibility (and tangibility) decouples the word from the neighbor in a way that helps to block its possible identification with the neighbor. To be sure, we receive the sacraments from the neighbor no less than we do the purely verbal proclamation of the gospel, but the affirmation of Christ's presence is focused on the elements and not on the one administering them. Most clearly in the eucharist, the declaration that *this* is Christ's body explicitly directs the attention of the communicant to the objective reality of the bread. If the bread is not sacrament apart from its being joined to a word, neither does the word in question mediate Jesus' presence apart from the bread. Once again, the freedom of Jesus' presence in the Spirit from physical constraint does not preclude its acquiring physical form; rather, the fact that it acquires such a ground is an expression of Jesus' freedom.[10]

CHRIST'S PRESENCE IN THE CHURCH

This last point opens up the second dimension of the way in which Christ encounters us. If talk of the Spirit expresses Christ's freedom, the fact that this Spirit comes to us in the specific forms of word and sacrament teaches us that this freedom is not arbitrary or formless. To paraphrase Karl Barth's famous remark, God's ability to speak to us through a pagan or an atheist does not license Christians to preach paganism or atheism.[11] Although God is free to address us in many ways, we have no freedom to speak of God beyond that which has been given us in and through Jesus of Nazareth. Inasmuch as we are able to recognize one another as persons in light of Jesus' having summoned us through word and sacrament, our lives as persons will be marked by an ongoing commitment to proclaim Jesus in word and sacrament.

It is important to emphasize once again that the effect of this proclamation is not only to bring us face to face with Jesus, but also to join us with the neighbor through whom Jesus calls us. Being baptized into the body of Christ is the affirmation of an individual's relationship both with Jesus and also with a wider community of human beings. This wider community is distinguished from other communities as church by its witness to Jesus' life, death, and resurrection in the con-

---

10. Cf. Frei, *Identity of Jesus Christ*, 194: "The Sacrament is not identical with [Christ's] physical presence . . . but it is the self-communication in physical form of one who is self-focused to us who cannot know self-focused presence except in physical form."

11. Barth, *CD* I/1, 55.

crete acts of word and sacrament. The need for such a witness follows from the fact that Jesus himself has ascended to the right hand of God and is therefore present in the world of space and time only indirectly, through the humanly mediated works of the Spirit. In this respect, the community's ministry is the provisional one of proclaiming Jesus' absence until he comes again (1 Cor. 11:26).

Yet the identity of the community is not exhausted by its sacramental witness, even if it is through this witness that the community is publicly identifiable as the church. For while the need for witness will end with Jesus' return, the life in community of which Jesus is the source and which is the aim of his ministry will not. Until Jesus' return, we encounter him only indirectly, as his Spirit claims us through our neighbor. From this perspective, it might seem that Jesus' return would render our neighbor superfluous; but the self-professed aim of Jesus' ministry is emphatically not that we should encounter him as an end in itself, as though our history had as its goal the final realization of his unmediated presence. Instead, Jesus' prayer to the God he calls Father is that his disciples "may be one, as we are one" (John 17:22). In the same way that the oneness of God is not that of an undifferentiated presence, but rather a perichoretic communion of three persons, so the concrete form of human unity in Christ is a function of our relation to all the other human persons with whom he is in relation.

As argued in chapter 4, the image of Jesus as the head of the body proves crucial for appreciating the way in which our relationships to Jesus and to our neighbors are interconnected. On the one hand, it is only by reference to Jesus that we are one body. Because he, as the head, gives the body its identity, to be part of this particular body means that "we must grow up in every way into him who is the head" (Eph. 4:15). On the other hand, the head is not the whole body: if the head is the source of growth, it nevertheless remains the case that the body's shape is determined by the arrangement of all its parts, each working in its place and knit to one another by a variety of joints that are distinct from the head (Eph. 4:16). In short, while the head identifies the body, the identity of the body is not reducible to the head. Consequently, just as it is impossible to be joined to the body without being under the head, so is it impossible to be in relationship with the head independently of the body's other members.

This dialectic between the church as witness to Christ's exalted life and as itself an aspect of that life reflects what Rowan Williams has described as "two irreducible moments" of God's work in history: on the one hand, the story of Jesus of Nazareth to which the church bears witness is the "unifying point of reference" for the community's life and as such is to be sharply distinguished from the community; on the other hand, "the necessarily unfinished ensemble of human stories drawn together" around this point is part and parcel of Jesus' own identity and thus itself a form of his presence.[12] These two moments are not parallel. The priority of the head over the members is reflected in the fact that the church's specific identity as the body of Christ is derived from its sharing in the body of Jesus offered in the eucharistic bread. As Paul argues, it is because there is one bread that "we who are many are one body, for we all partake of the one bread" (1 Cor. 10:17). Correspondingly, to fail to recognize this unilateral dependence of the ecclesial body on the eucharistic body is not only to come under judgment, but also to cut oneself off from the life of the body in a way that leaves one vulnerable to sickness and death (1 Cor. 11:27–30).

In this way, the church's life as the communion *of* saints is possible only because the church is first of all a place of communion *in* the holy things of water, bread, and wine: both these images need to be held together as complementary translations of the creedal *communio sanctorum.* Yet this insistence that the church is unilaterally dependent for its existence on the prior action of God in Jesus does not undermine (and is, indeed, the basis for) the claim that Jesus' identity is inseparable from the church. While the church is publicly identifiable by its witness to Jesus, it is not possible fully to identify Jesus without reference to those who, through the action of his Spirit, now form part of his story. Moreover, because that story will be completed only at the end of history, the fullness of Jesus' identity as the Christ has yet to be revealed, even if the fact that Jesus is the Christ has been established by his having been raised to God's right hand.[13] In this context, there is reason to take seriously the fact that the Apostles'

---

12. Rowan Williams, *On Christian Theology* (Oxford: Blackwell, 2000), 172.

13. "Only the telling of the whole story [of a person] delivers the truth of the person; and of no person is this more true than Jesus Christ. For he is known only as he is received in the community to which the Spirit is given, so that only in telling the stories of all its members can his story fully be told" (Gerard Loughlin, "The Basis and Authority of Doctrine," in *The Cambridge Companion to Christian Doctrine,* ed. Colin E. Gunton [Cambridge: Cambridge University Press, 1997], 53).

Creed speaks of the resurrection of the *body* (singular), reflecting the church's expectation of the eschatological revelation of the one body of Christ in its entirety as head and members.

CHRIST'S PRESENCE
OUTSIDE OF THE CHURCH

In parallel with what has been said earlier, the affirmation of the church as a form of Christ's presence must not be taken to imply that Christ is present only in or for church members. As Alistair McFadyen has argued, "Christ is not only present *in* the Church, structuring its internal communications, but also stands *between* the Church and its world, structuring its missionary communication."[14] Here, too, the church's identity as the body of Christ needs to be subordinated to its role as witness to a Jesus whose presence is *not* capable of being circumscribed by any particular category or group of people.[15] Because human personhood is a matter of divine decision that precedes any human act, it cannot be viewed as a quality that is dependent on any such act, including the act of baptism (see Mark 16:16). In bearing witness to Jesus, the church also bears witness to this fact, with the paradoxical result that it can be understood as a form of Jesus' presence only so long as it points away from itself to Jesus. In other words, its public identity as the body of Christ is not based on any qualities of its own, but on its recognition that it has no such qualities that might be claimed as an advantage over against outsiders.

Douglas Farrow has argued that the church's relation to the world is characterized by a combination of continuity and discontinuity: in looking to the Savior who is absent, the church stands apart from the world; but because the Savior to whom it looks is the Jesus who has suffered and been glorified in the flesh, the church continues to live for the world.[16] It is important to add that this commitment to the world is not a matter of condescension, charity, or even of obligation, to the extent that any of these terms might be taken to suggest that

---

14. Alistair I. McFadyen, *The Call to Personhood: A Christian Theory of the Individual in Social Relationships* (Cambridge: Cambridge University Press, 1990), 201.

15. See Frei, *Identity of Jesus Christ*, 189–90.

16. Douglas Farrow, *Ascension and Ecclesia: On the Significance of the Doctrine of the Ascension for Ecclesiology and Christian Cosmology* (Edinburgh: Clark, 1999), 80.

the church confronts the world from a position of advantage. To be sure, the church operates from the belief that it has "news" to preach that is "good" for those outside its boundaries to hear, but it has no way of assessing whether the gospel it preaches is the good news of Jesus Christ (and not merely a manifestation of its own communal self-interest) independently of its encounter with those on its outside. If the content of the gospel can be summarized as the declaration that God in Christ has addressed all human beings as persons, the fact that it is Jesus alone who continues in and through his Spirit to teach the church who and what persons are means that the precise meaning of the gospel is a matter of ongoing discovery for those within the community no less than for those outside.

The dependence on Jesus for our identities as persons rules out the idea that human beings are guarantors of their own identities—least of all of their identities as Christians. Rowan Williams has pointed out that the illusory character of human self-determination is disclosed in Peter's all-too-quickly discredited insistence (cited in all four Gospels) on his willingness to follow Jesus to prison and death. That he eventually does prove able to follow Jesus to death (as foretold in John 21:18–19) is evidently not attributable to any capacity of his own, but solely to the fact that Jesus continues to claim him in spite of his obvious inadequacies (cf. Luke 22:31–32). So more broadly, the identity Christians have is precisely not one they can claim for themselves, but rather, "entire gift, new creation; not generated from their effort or reflection or even their conscious desire."[17]

If our identity is "entire gift," then it is never something that can be treated as ontological leverage over against non-Christians. It follows that in proclaiming to others the call of Jesus Christ, the Christian should not suppose to be authorized to tell others who they are.[18] Only Jesus as God's own Word incarnate is able to tell others who they are. The evangelist has no such capacity. Indeed, in light of the ongoing character of Jesus' story, Christians cannot say fully who they themselves are, still less define the being of others. After all, the gospel is primarily about who Jesus is, and only then and in that light about

---

17. Williams, *On Christian Theology*, 270.
18. Ann Dummett has argued that the presumption of telling people who they are is a defining feature of oppression (*A Portrait of English Racism*, 2nd ed. [CARAF Publications, 1984], 150; cited in Williams, *On Christian Theology*, 280).

ourselves. The church that is faithful in its proclamation will therefore
not presume to define the other any more than it will presume to
define itself, but rather will conceive of its task quite modestly as that
of pointing to Jesus as the only one capable of defining human identity.

This claim may seem exaggerated at best and self-deceived at worst.
After all, isn't it true that the church baptizes people in repentance for
the forgiveness of sins? And doesn't it thereby define the one baptized
as a sinner, and those who have been baptized as forgiven sinners?
The answer to these questions is that while the church certainly baptizes, it does not (or at least ought not) presume on that basis to
define anybody's status before God. On the contrary, the sacrament
of baptism is the church's confession that because the one baptized
has been claimed by God in Christ, neither the church nor any other
created power has the authority to define her identity. In submitting
to Christian baptism, the individual implicitly assents to this conviction, and thereby confesses that she, too, is incapable of securing her
own identity—but she certainly does not transfer this power to the
church. Rather, she joins the church's confession that her identity as
a person is guaranteed by God alone. While the fact of baptism distinguishes Christians from non-Christians sociologically, theologically
speaking, baptism has less to do with claiming a particular identity for
oneself than surrendering such claims before the sovereignty of the
risen Christ.

A similar line of reasoning applies to the issue of categorizing non-
Christians as sinners. Leaving aside the basic theological point that
the individual's status as a sinner is not a legitimate criterion on the
basis of which to distinguish Christians from non-Christians, it is far
from clear that the act of preaching the gospel entails the prior conviction of those to whom it is preached as sinners. Bonhoeffer was
unsparing in his attacks on preaching that thought its first task was
to show human beings a need, difficulty, or weakness to which the
gospel provided an answer.[19] Without seeking to minimize either the
fact or the seriousness of human sin, Bonhoeffer stressed that Jesus'
practice took the form of challenging people's strengths rather than

---

19. "It's not the least necessary to spy out things; the Bible never does so" (letter of
8 July 1944, in *Letters and Papers from Prison*, ed. Eberhard Bethge [New York: Macmillan,
1971], 345). See also the letters of 8 and 30 June 1944.

exploiting their weaknesses.[20] Jesus' harsh words to the Pharisees, for example, were directed against the piety they claimed for themselves and not to sniffing out and exposing their secret sins (Matt. 23:1–5, 16–36). Here, as elsewhere, Jesus confronted people where they placed themselves and did not attempt to claim an advantage over them by belittling them.

That the refusal to define my neighbor applies to those outside no less than to those within the community of faith follows from the conclusions reached at the end of the last chapter: I should regard my neighbor as someone who serves me by providing the God-given occasion for living out my own identity as a person rather than as someone under obligation to me (see Rom. 1:14–15). For this reason, it is necessary to confess that Christ's presence in the lives of those who have acknowledged his claim on them is balanced by a corresponding presence among those who have not. Jesus claims the non-Christian no less than her Christian counterpart, though she does not yet acknowledge this claim. Her significance for the church lies precisely in her being outside the church, and thus as one before whom Christ summons those within the church to live out their identities as persons. As a neighbor, the non-Christian is the one through whom Christ is present to the Christian. Indeed, insofar as the God of Jesus is noted for the habit of choosing those who lack any special claim to consideration, there is every reason to expect that Christians will find Christ's presence outside the church's boundaries more decisive in shaping their own lives as persons—and thus the life of the church as Christ's body—than what takes place within the community of faith.[21]

This latter possibility lies at the heart of the sermon at Nazareth that Luke portrays as the first public event in Jesus' ministry (Luke 4:16–30). In order to appreciate the significance of this story, it is important to remember that Nazareth was a small town in "Galilee of the Gentiles." Its population would have been neither wealthy nor influential, and passages elsewhere in the Gospels suggest that the fact that Jesus hailed from such a place cast a shadow over his ministry (John 1:46; 7:41, 52). It is thus reasonable to suppose that the people Jesus

---

20. "When Jesus blessed sinners, they were real sinners, but Jesus did not make everyone a sinner first. He called them away from their sin, not into their sin" (letter of 8 June 1944, in *Letters and Papers*, 341).

21. Cf. Frei's interpretation of Romans 9–11 in *Identity of Jesus Christ*, 192.

addresses in Luke 4 would have regarded themselves as marginalized with respect to the official Judaism of the Jerusalem temple.

To such people, the words that Jesus is recorded as having read from Isaiah would have been good news. The text describes the social transformation of the Jubilee ("the year of the Lord's favor"), which is depicted in the Old Testament as an occasion for reversing the accumulated effects of social marginalization. Though the degree to which the practices of the fifty-year Jubilee cycle were ever carried out is debated, the relevant injunctions hold out the goal of undoing the cumulative effects of inequality and want: debts were to be remitted, land returned to its ancestral owners, and (Hebrew) slaves released from bondage (Lev. 25:8–55). As projected by Isaiah to the final time of God's eschatological reign, the year of favor becomes a trope for a time when poverty, disability, captivity, and oppression would be no more.

This background makes it easy to understand why Jesus' declaration that Isaiah's prophecy has been fulfilled would find a welcome response (v. 22). At that point, however, Jesus does a very strange thing: he juxtaposes these words of promise spoken to Israel's marginalized (and, therefore, to the congregants assembled before him) with biblical passages that speak instead of God's grace to non-Israelites:

> There were many widows in Israel in the time of Elijah, when the heaven was shut up for three years and six months, and there was a severe famine over all the land; yet Elijah was sent to none of them except to a widow at Zarephath in Sidon. There were also many lepers in Israel in the time of the prophet Elisha, and none of them was cleansed except Naaman the Syrian. (Luke 4:25–27)

It is rather as though Jesus had concluded a sermon to a group of poor white sharecroppers by telling them that blacks were the objects of God's special concern. Small wonder that the good people of Nazareth responded by forming a lynch mob (vv. 28–29).

In order to appreciate the violence of this reaction, it is important to note that Jesus isn't simply asking his audience to be more inclusive in their outlook by acknowledging that Gentiles might have a share in eschatological blessing alongside Israel. In light of prophetic texts like Isa. 2:2–4 and 56:6–8, there is no reason to suppose that such a message would in itself have been controversial. The shocking thing about Jesus' sermon is rather that he seems to be telling his compatriots that the inclusion of outsiders may overshadow their own. It is not simply that non-Israelites will eventually find a place in God's plan, but that they may well turn out to be at the very center of God's redeeming activity.

This is not to say that Israel in general or the citizens of Nazareth in particular are simply rejected. Jesus nowhere denies that his compatriots are included in Isaiah's promises; but he does suggest that Israel's God is often most tellingly active among those who have no claim to divine grace. Insofar as this story continues to be regarded by Christians as part of the good news that they are asked to hear, it requires a similar acknowledgement that God's activity in Christ may turn out to be most powerfully present in encounter with persons outside the recognized boundaries of the church. Once again, the fact of having been addressed by God in Christ is not grounds for the claiming of certain "rights" over against God or other people, but rather an occasion to recognize God's commitment precisely to those who have no rights.

DISCERNMENT AND FAITHFULNESS

In a section of his Corinthian correspondence to which I have already had occasion to refer, Paul stresses the importance of discerning the body of Christ in the eucharistic elements (1 Cor. 11:29). The need for discernment implies that the presence of the body is not obvious. In the previous chapter I argued that we encounter our neighbor only through Jesus, and in this chapter I have tried to make sense of this requirement in light of the fact that Jesus' presence among us is not obvious. Christians confess that Jesus is ascended in the flesh to the right hand of God and thus fundamentally absent. If Christians wish to claim at the same time that we encounter his body in the eucharistic bread, in the community of the baptized, and even in those who are outside that community, then discernment is clearly called for. What does it entail?

It entails first of all that we recognize that Jesus' ascension means his freedom from every attempt to limit or control his presence either physically or conceptually. In his earthly life Jesus refused every possi-

bility of securing his own identity. Instead, he handed over his identity
to God, who in the resurrection secured it against all powers that presume to define it for their own purposes. At the same time, however,
the Christian confession of Jesus' freedom is misunderstood, if not be-
lied, if it is spiritualized as a diffuse sort of omnipresence. If the risen
Jesus continues to be present through his Spirit, this Spirit is not free-
floating. Rather, it is an expression of Jesus' freedom as the Word of
God; and Jesus, who sits at God's right hand, is the one who sends
it on his followers until he comes again to judge the living and the
dead. It follows that the gift of the Spirit should not be interpreted to
mean that we can find Jesus everywhere and anywhere, as though he
were now at our disposal. On the contrary, as gift, the Spirit reminds
us that we meet Jesus only where he wills, because as the risen one,
he is no longer at our disposal.

But if Jesus' freedom is not subject to our control, neither is it arbitrary. In his freedom he addresses us as persons and thereby calls
us to be with him as he is with us. This address comes to us as the
Spirit, through our neighbor, names us persons (in baptism) and summons us to live as persons (in the eucharist). Because it comes to us
entirely from without ourselves, our personhood is not something we
can claim on our own merit. Consequently, there is no basis for the
supposition that the gift of personhood, once received, might be deployed as ontological capital over against either God or our neighbor.
The gift of personhood is strictly a function of God's having addressed
us in Christ and cannot be detached from the encounter that such
address implies; and because Christ's presence with us in the time between ascension and parousia is indirect, encountering him requires
discernment.

This need for discernment is clearly shown by Jesus' insistence that
his presence cannot be conjured by cries of "Lord, Lord" (Matt. 7:21–
23). The promise that all who seek will find, that all who ask will
receive, and that the door will be opened to all who knock does not
take away the necessity of performing the concrete acts of seeking,
asking, and knocking. That Jesus speaks to us in the power of the
Spirit is a promise that we neither can nor need earn; but that does
not make it any less important for us faithfully to attend to his speech.
Discernment is an integral part of such faithful listening, because it is
of the essence of faithfulness that we are unable to specify in advance

precisely what it may entail. Far from permitting an attitude of indolence, faithfulness requires alertness to the possibility of unforeseen developments (see, e.g., Matt. 25:13; Luke 12:41–46).

At this point the objection might be raised that it is Jesus' faithfulness and not our own that is decisive (2 Tim. 2:13). Yet because the form of Jesus' faithfulness is no more predictable than our own, the affirmation of his fidelity in the face of our unfaithfulness in no way lessens the need for faithful discernment on our part. Jesus' faithfulness is not an abstract or self-contained metaphysical principle, but a (personal!) commitment to lead us to the life with the Father in the Spirit that he himself enjoys as God's own Word. As David Ford notes, if Jesus' presence can be described as "vague," this "is not so much because of abstraction or generality but because of the utter particularity of this face's relation to each face."[22] This particularity is such that he meets us where we are; but though we do not have to go anywhere to find him, we can certainly fail to acknowledge him when he finds us.

According to Jesus, his ongoing presence is inextricably bound up with our neighbors (see Matt. 25:41–45). Paul echoes this same point when he speaks of encountering Christ as a matter of discerning his body, since this body is irreducibly social in character. Though the glorified humanity of the exalted Christ is absent, his body is not limited to this one human being, even though it is he (as the "head") who gives this body its identity. Insofar as Christ's body "names a place where God locates God's own self," it is present wherever Christ is encountered, whether inside or (following Aquinas's insight that Christ is the head of all humankind) outside the church.[23]

As noted earlier, these encounters are not the outcome of trying to discern Christ in the face of the neighbor. Such attempts only occlude the particularity of the neighbor and thus Christ's own particularity as the risen and exalted one who cannot be treated as a fixed datum against which other people can be matched. If encounter with Christ is truly to be an encounter, and not merely the projection of my own preconceptions, discernment must not be interpreted as a process of

---

22. David Ford, *Self and Salvation: Being Transformed* (Cambridge: Cambridge University Press, 1999), 175–76.
23. Eugene F. Rogers Jr., *Sexuality and the Christian Body: Their Way into the Triune God* (Oxford: Blackwell, 1999), 240.

my trying to perceive my neighbor in a particular way. Rather than *my* effort to see Christ in the neighbor, discernment is better understood as my openness to *Christ's* work of disclosing the neighbor to me. And because the distinctions that shape any encounter between Christ, my neighbor, and myself are experienced only in the context of a particular social setting, my inability to encounter the neighbor apart from Christ is matched by an inability to encounter the risen Christ apart from a concrete human neighbor. In short, the Jesus who meets me *in* my neighbor meets me only *together with* my neighbor.[24]

In this way, personal encounter is given a distinctive shape. I do not recognize the neighbor's personhood by a process of extrapolation from my own (or, what amounts to the same thing, from my idea of what it means to be a person). Quite the contrary, it is the recognition that my neighbor has been addressed as a person by God in Christ that is the basis for my always evolving understanding of what (or, better, who) a person is. Importantly, this holds true whether or not I am cast in the role of recipient of my neighbor's testimony to Christ (in listening to a sermon, for example) or am the one who gives this testimony; in either situation, Christ meets me as the one who has already claimed the neighbor. In the first case, the idea that Christ claims me as a person is implicitly rooted in the conviction that he has already so claimed the one addressing me. In the second, it is only in the attempt to articulate Christ's claim to my neighbor (an attempt that cannot be evaluated apart from the neighbor's response) that I myself encounter Christ as anything other than a projection of my own imagination. Either way, it is only on the basis of my recognition of Christ's address to the neighbor—and the encounter with the neighbor as a person that such recognition entails—that I find myself addressed as well.

As the one who is crucified yet risen, Jesus manifests in the Spirit a stubborn difference that resists our efforts at domestication. And while this difference is rooted in the freedom of Jesus' exaltation to God's right hand, it is manifested within time and space in the freedom of his Spirit, who, as the mediator of Jesus' presence in word and

---

24. As Rogers notes, "The I-Thou phenomenology tends to reduce co-humanity to co-individuality....Christ promises to be with human beings not each individually that we might meet him as I and Thou, but when *two or three* are *already* gathered in his name" (*Sexuality and the Christian Body*, 184).

sacrament, discloses him as irreducibly other than and outside of the self in the face of the neighbor. To encounter Christ is therefore to encounter a body, something (or, rather, someone) exterior to myself; and if this fact of embodiment cannot be made part of the definition of what it means to be a person (since neither the first nor the third persons of the Trinity are embodied), it is nevertheless a distinctive feature of the personhood of God's Word, and therefore of all those who are persons in him. Indeed, the social and bodily character of our discernment of Christ may be interpreted as the creaturely form of the intratrinitarian correlation of personhood with difference: just as the personhood of Father, Son, and Spirit refers to that which they do not hold in common, so our identity as persons in Christ rests on the Spirit's naming us as distinct both from Jesus and from each other.

From this perspective, Jesus' status as our permanent representative before God does not entail the contradiction of our personhood that Sölle fears. Jesus holds us a place as the head in relation to whom the various members have their place as parts of a body with a particular form. This role is permanent, because in the absence of the head the members, far from acquiring increased autonomy, simply lack the context that gives them their specific identity. Yet the role of the head does not render any of the members superfluous: if the members have no life apart from the head, the head is no less incomplete apart from the rest of the body, without which it loses its own distinctive identity as head. When the category of representation is interpreted within this somatic metaphor, Jesus' role of holding a place for us before God is seen to be fully consistent with the possibility of our occupying that place.

At this point, however, it might be objected that the body metaphor allows for difference only at the price of introducing hierarchy. Granted that Paul develops his image of the body's many members by citing the diversity of the Spirit's gifts within the community, doesn't the way he describes these various callings invariably introduce distinctions of higher and lower, greater and less (as in, e.g., 1 Cor. 12:27–30)? Here one might quite legitimately point out the fundamentally conservative effect that the interpretation of the church as Christ's body has had over the centuries. While the image of the body allows the presence of diversity within the church to be acknowledged and even celebrated, the distinctions between different members has regularly been understood to imply a hierarchical ordering that carries with it profoundly unequal access to social goods. As a result of this process, difference ends up being subverted by being interpreted in terms of fixed, strictly defined, and carefully managed roles within the larger whole. While the beginnings of this process are already visible within the New Testament, the next chapter explores how a chris-tological deepening of the body metaphor can block these socially conservative moves.

– 7 –

Human Relationships
and Reciprocity

The last two chapters have discussed human relationships within the
context of the Pauline image of the body of Christ. While attention
was given to the ways in which relationships with others shape an individual's identity as a person, the discussion remained on a fairly general
level, with little reference to the concrete forms of difference that define otherness. The time has now come to ask how particular forms of
difference affect our understanding of other persons as members of the
one body of Christ. Specifically, is it possible to take the differences
between persons seriously without seeing them as manifestations of a
hierarchically ordered series?

There can be little question that within the New Testament the
image of the church as the body of Christ is often interpreted in hierarchical terms. At the same time, however, it is important to keep in
mind that the body is not the only image used by the biblical writers to
characterize human existence in Christ. Nor does the biblical witness
anywhere suggest that life in Christ involves the obliteration of one's
identity. On the contrary, the new names that Jesus himself bestows
on some of his followers (Mark 3:16–17) implies that his claiming of
human beings actually brings out the distinctiveness of their identities. Likewise, the sovereignty of Jesus as head of the body does not
prevent him from taking on the role of a servant (John 13:3–5; cf.
Matt. 20:28 and pars.) or calling his disciples friends rather than slaves
(John 15:15).

These more egalitarian features of the New Testament witness do
not in any way mitigate human beings' unilateral dependence on Jesus
as the source of their personhood, but it does make it more difficult
to interpret the language of head and members in exclusively hierar-

chical terms. In this context, it is significant that within the Pauline corpus itself the description of the church as the body of Christ is supplemented by its characterization as Christ's spouse. While the relationship of husband and wife is certainly also open to a narrowly hierarchical interpretation, we will see that the claim made in Ephesians 5 that this relationship ought to be interpreted christologically has the effect of calling established hierarchies into question. Before moving to a detailed study of the Ephesians text, however, it is necessary to make some preliminary remarks on the relationship between equality and difference in light of the christological determination of human personhood.

INTERPERSONAL RELATIONS: EQUALITY IN CHRIST

Insofar as all human beings find their identity as persons in Jesus, it is both possible and necessary to say that they are all equal in Christ (see 1 Cor. 12:13; Gal. 3:26–28). As already noted, this equality in and under Christ is the basis upon which human beings are able to stand before God. For though human beings have as creatures no natural share in the eternal communion of the divine three persons, God gives them a share by taking flesh in Jesus and addressing to us the same Word that defines God's own triune life.

As argued in the last chapter, the dependence of each and every human person on Jesus entails a commitment to the neighbor as the one in whom Jesus encounters us and to whom he directs us. This thoroughgoing interdependence of human persons undermines the possibility that some people might be conceived as ontologically superior to or nearer Jesus than others. This point finds ancillary support in Jesus' repeated insistence on the need to forgive one's neighbor (Matt. 6:12, 14–15; 18:21–35 and pars.; Mark 11:25; Luke 6:37). Evidently, forgiveness is integral to life in communion with God; and insofar as Jesus implies by the scope of his command that all are equal both with respect to their need for forgiveness and in their capacity to grant it, he leaves no basis for claiming advantage over one's neighbor.

At the same time, because this equality is based on Jesus' claim and not on the particular characteristic of individuals, the category of equality is of only very limited use in formulating rules for our relationships with others. If the only constant I can identify in the many neighbors whom I meet is Jesus' commitment to them, then I do not have much ground on which to construct an ethic. This is not to say that the differences between people relativize the force of particular injunctions. Prohibitions against murder, theft, adultery, slander, and the like continue to mark out the basic conditions necessary if people are to live together. The problem is that such rules provide only very limited guidance in articulating the positive content of my relationship with my neighbor. Granted, for example, that the commandment to love my neighbor applies with equal force in my relationship with my wife, my daughter, and the couple who live next door, fidelity to that commandment will mean very different things in each of these three cases.

As the last example suggests, the christological basis of our equality as persons allows the enormous range of differences between persons to be taken seriously. Insofar as our status as persons lies entirely in the fact of our having been claimed as such by Jesus, our individual particularity cannot be viewed as peripheral to some common core of personhood, but instead must be interpreted as an inseparable feature of our personal identities. And because Jesus points us to the other who is different from ourselves as a constant check on our conceptions of personhood, we have no choice but to treat each other in ways that reflect and honor those differences. To do otherwise would amount to denying the christological basis of personal existence in favor of some rival account. The challenge lies in finding a way to affirm these differences that is consistent with the equality of all persons in Christ.

INTERPERSONAL RELATIONS: DIFFERENCE IN CHRIST

On one level the affirmation of difference bespeaks nothing more than the commonsense observation that equality is not a matter of interchangeability: if we are all one body, we are not all part of the body in the same way (1 Cor. 12:19). In this context, it is worth noting that in scripture the identification of God as no respecter of persons (see, e.g., Rom. 2:11; Eph. 6:9; 1 Pet. 1:17) is established over the course of a narrative in which particular persons emerge as the object of God's special concern. In other words, God's overall impartiality takes concrete form in particular acts of divine partisanship, in which the lowly are raised up and the mighty brought low (see, e.g., Deut. 7:7–8; Ps. 107:39–41; Luke 1:52; 1 Cor. 1:27–29; cf. Job 12:13–25; John 9:1–3; Rom. 9:6–13; 11:11–12, 25–32). Nor is this fact especially surprising. Given the broad spectrum of physical conditions under which human beings live, it makes sense that their fundamental equality before God can be affirmed only by attending to the differences among them in a way that favors those whose equal status is under threat.

On one level, these acts of divine partiality can be seen as a temporary expedient designed to bring everyone to the same level. This is certainly the impression given by the parables of the laborers in the vineyard (Matt. 20:1–16) and the prodigal son (Luke 15:11–32). Yet attention to the biblical witness taken as a whole makes it clear that bringing everyone to the same level does not mean making everyone the same. For example, God does not raise Israelites to equality with the Egyptians by integrating them more fully into Egyptian society; on the contrary, God calls them out of Egypt to their own destiny (see Amos 9:7). In this way, election certainly entails the overthrow of those aspects of individual and collective identity (viz., the Israelites' status as slaves) that stand in the way of human beings fulfilling their calling as persons, but it is not a summons to homogeneity. Already in the Old Testament one finds the belief that the eschatological goal of God's saving work is a world in which each nation has its own place, such that "Israel will be the third with Egypt and Assyria, a blessing in the midst of the earth" (Isa. 19:24; see also v. 25). In this context, the temptation that constitutes the greatest threat to Israel's calling is precisely its desire to be like other nations (1 Sam. 8:4–8, 20; 2 Kings 17:15; Ezek. 20:30–32).

Jesus' practice of associating with "tax collectors and sinners" (Matt. 9:11; 11:19 and pars.; cf. 21:31–32) reflects this same selective affirmation of difference. Though he repeatedly crosses those boundaries of gender, occupation, illness, confessional or ethnic identity, and sin that were used to exclude certain people from full participation in the life of the covenant community, his attitude toward the differences these boundaries mark is varied. In some cases he eliminates them (so that the sick are healed and sinners forgiven), but in other cases he allows them to stand (Gentiles are not made Jews, nor women men).[1] Nor does he justify his activities by a consistent appeal to some underlying anthropology: if in certain cases he points to the fact that a particular individual is a member of the chosen people (Luke 13:16; 19:9), in others he explicitly calls into question the eschatological significance of a person's ethnic affiliation (Matt. 8:11–12 and par.; cf. Matt. 3:9 and par.). In the same vein, he does not deny that those to whom he offers forgiveness are sinners; instead, he proclaims that their sin is no longer an obstacle to participation in God's realm (Matt. 9:10–13 and pars.).

In short, while Jesus regularly undermines the social divisions that exclude certain categories of people from full participation in the covenant community, he does not promote a homogenization in which all people are made to conform more closely to some preestablished norm. If he had, it is doubtful that his ministry would have stirred up the controversy depicted in the Gospels, for greater homogeneity seems to have been precisely what Jesus' theological opponents sought. The Pharisees, too, were interested in affirming God's call to the whole of Israel, including "tax collectors and sinners"; it might even extend as far as the Gentiles (see Matt. 23:15).[2] For the Pharisees, however, responding to this call meant conforming to the demands of the law, including a process of repentance, restitution, and renewed commitment for those guilty of transgressing those demands, and a formal procedure of incorporation into the covenant community for non-Jews. By contrast, Jesus associates with Jewish sinners, Samaritans, and Gentiles quite apart from their commitment to any such process. It is therefore hardly surprising that his declarations of forgiveness are viewed by onlookers as an unwarranted usurping of divine prerogatives (Mark 2:5–7 and pars.; Luke 7:36–50).[3]

That Jesus would have proclaimed the fullness of God's realm not

---

1. See chapter 8 for further discussion of this topic.

2. As E. P. Sanders has rightly stressed, "The Pharisees ... may have held aloof from ordinary people, but ... all the evidence is against the assumption that the Pharisees would feel hostile to including ordinary people in the kingdom." As far as the status of sinners was concerned, the Pharisees shared the "universal [Jewish] view that forgiveness is *always* available to those who return to the Lord" (E. P. Sanders, *Jesus and Judaism* [London: SCM, 1985], 199, 202).

3. Sanders argues that Jesus' message was distinctive precisely because he "offered [sinners] inclusion in the kingdom not only *while they were still sinners* but also without requiring repentance as normally understood" (*Jesus and Judaism*, 206).

only to the "poor" whose devotion to the law would have been suspect in the eyes of the pious, but also to the wicked who deliberately flouted the commandments explains something of the scandal his ministry seems to have produced. Indeed, this same sense of scandal soon seems to have afflicted the majority of his followers. For although Paul speaks provocatively of the justification of the ungodly (Rom. 4:5), nowhere either in his letters or in the other New Testament letters do we find any indication that early Christians either practiced or encouraged the kind of indiscriminate table fellowship for which Jesus appears to have been notorious. If anything, the evidence suggests that such fellowship was discouraged (see, e.g., 1 Cor. 5:2; 2 Cor. 6:14; 2 John 10–11; but cf. Gal. 2:11–14).

Yet even if Jesus' own practice of associating with sinners was soon eclipsed in the early church, the idea that an individual's stance before God depended solely on her or his relationship with Jesus remained a central Christian conviction. When Paul claimed that Jesus was humanity's righteousness (1 Cor. 1:30; cf. Rom. 1:17; 3:21–22), he meant that a human being was declared to be righteous (i.e., "right" with God) on the basis of her or his relationship to Jesus rather than owing to any particular moral qualities or achievements (Rom. 10:9; 2 Cor. 5:21; Phil. 3:8–9; cf. Acts 4:12).

While the Pauline doctrine of justification certainly implies that the particular characteristics and circumstances that differentiate one human being from another play no role in determining whether or not someone *is* a person, the conclusion does not follow that such differences are irrelevant to one's capacity to live out one's calling *as* a person. The categorization of all physical and social differences as matters indifferent does not accord with Jesus' insistence that his followers not model their life together on worldly hierarchies (see, e.g., Matt. 20:25–28 and pars.; 23:8–12). Still more to the point, it is hard to explain why Jesus bothered to give sight to the blind or heal the sick if such factors had no bearing on an individual's personhood. That he found it necessary to straighten the woman with the bent back (Luke 13:10–13), for example, suggests that the realm Jesus proclaims is not one in which spiritual status can be neatly distinguished from the concrete conditions of life in the body.

Because Jesus claims the whole human being, body and soul, answering his call requires an openness to changing one's physical no less than one's spiritual condition. Such changes may include leaving work and family (Matt. 4:18–22 and pars.; cf. 10:37 and par.), doing without a fixed abode (Matt. 8:19–20 and par.), or selling one's possessions (Matt. 19:21 and pars.). That the particular shape this response will take will vary with the individual concerned is a theme echoed by Paul, who notes that "each has a particular gift [*charisma*] from God, one having one kind and another a different kind" (1 Cor. 7:7). While careful to affirm that one's ethnic or social status in no way determines one's status as a person (1 Cor. 7:19–21a), Paul nevertheless allows that a Christian slave who has the opportunity to obtain freedom should make use of it (v. 21b), and he gives a specifically christological rationale for this injunction: "you were bought with a price; do not become slaves of human masters" (v. 23). In this way, the principle that material circumstances can neither establish nor destroy one's personhood is shown to be compatible with an insistence that one cannot fulfill one's calling as a person in utter disregard of those circumstances. One may be a person in Christ as a Jew or a Gentile, but knowing what it means to be a person as a Jew or a Gentile requires careful and continuous reflection.

Granted that the physical shape of Christian callings differs from one person to another, the question of the relationship between different callings is unavoidable. As the apostle who first preached the gospel to the Corinthians, Paul claims a certain kind of authority over them (1 Cor. 4:15; 9:2; 2 Cor. 13:10) that justifies his giving them very concrete directives. Inasmuch as not everyone is an apostle (1 Cor. 12:28–29), Paul's vision of equality before God clearly cannot be interpreted as an egalitarianism in which everyone has an equal say within the church. The differences that are part and parcel of our existence as distinct members of Christ's body take concrete physical (male and female, circumcised and uncircumcised, children and adults) and social (slave and free, clergy and laity, married and single) forms that raise important questions about how human beings should relate to one another. Much of Paul's own correspondence represents his various attempts to answer such questions as they surfaced in the experience of particular Christian communities.

Even though Paul's letters are directed to particular congregations facing a wide range of issues, certain basic themes govern his responses. Consideration for the weak, for example, is a prominent feature in his correspondence (Rom. 14:1–9; 15:1–6; 1 Cor. 8:7–13; 12:22–26; Gal. 6:1–2; 1 Thess. 5:14; cf. Matt. 18:6, 10 and pars.) that suggests a general desire to diffuse tensions between groups in order to build up the church in unity (cf. 1 Cor. 11:17–22; 14:1–12; Phil. 1:27; 4:2–3). Yet Paul also makes it clear that there are definite limits to what can be tolerated, especially when it comes to practices that attempt to suppress differences between individual members as a means of bearing collective witness to equality in Christ. This resistance to the homogenization of the church is manifest in Paul's trenchant opposition to the circumcision of Gentile converts (Gal. 2:3–5; 5:2–12; Phil. 3:2–3; cf. 1 Cor. 7:18–19), as well as in his resistance to practices that appear to him to blur the distinction between men and women (1 Cor. 11:2–16; cf. 14:33b–35).

Though Paul is remarkably consistent in his refusal to interpret equality in Christ with homogeneity, the effects of this affirmation of difference on the shape of Christian practice are by no means uniform. Paul's resistance to demands for the circumcision of Gentile converts served to undermine any notion of hierarchy in the relationship between Jewish and Gentile Christians (Rom. 1:16; 2:9–11).[4] Whether or not a man was circumcised was irrelevant to his status as a person in Christ, and thus was not allowed to serve as a criterion for exclusion or inclusion in the church (Gal. 2:11–16). The effect of Paul's stance in this context is thus profoundly egalitarian.[5]

By contrast, Paul's resistance to the blurring of distinctions between women and men appears to have had a decidedly less revolutionary effect. To be sure, the discussion of women's headgear in 1 Cor. 11:2–16 does not have as its aim the restriction of women's roles in the church. On the contrary, Paul's aim in this passage is to describe the conditions under which women may take up the crucial tasks of prayer and prophecy (v. 5). Nevertheless, the strategy Paul uses to make his case seemingly grounds the distinction between man and woman in an ontological hierarchy that places man is above woman as her "head" (1 Cor. 11:3; cf. vv. 7–9). Although Paul himself goes some way toward

---

4. Though Paul attributes to Jews a certain priority in salvation history (Rom. 9:4; cf. 3:2), there is no hint that this translates into any functional superiority of Jews over Gentiles in the church.

5. In light of later Christian anti-Semitism, it is worth noting that Paul anticipates and rejects the claim of Gentile superiority in Rom. 11:13–32.

subverting the hierarchical implications of this line of reasoning by affirming that "woman cannot do without man, neither can man do without woman in the Lord" (1 Cor. 11:11, JB),[6] the church soon came to accept the explicit subordination of women to men as consistent with Paul's teaching (see, e.g., 1 Tim. 2:9–15; Titus 2:3–5). These hierarchical models of relationships between human persons raise the question of how the affirmation of genuine difference between human beings is to be reconciled with the idea that all human beings in Christ are equally persons.

ADDRESSING THE PROBLEM OF GENDER RELATIONS

Karl Barth argued that the biblical account of human creation as male and female established gender difference as the defining feature of humanity.[7] Given the degree to which gender competes with a variety of other features in shaping our sense of identity as human beings, it is open to question whether quite so sweeping a conclusion is justified. Even if gender is not the fundamental feature of human being, however, it does serve in much of scripture as a paradigmatic context for describing the implications of difference for understanding the character of human beings' relationships with God and each other. It certainly functions in this way in the letter to the Ephesians, where it is written that the joining of man and woman as "one flesh" described in Genesis 2 is a "mystery" that refers to "Christ and the church" (Eph. 5:32). In other words, if our life as persons is established through our relationship with Christ, that most crucial of relationships is reflected in the joining of a man and a woman in marriage.

---

6. Though Elisabeth Schüssler Fiorenza argues that the goal of Paul's argument in 1 Cor. 11:2–16 "is not the reinforcement of gender differences," the fact that Paul here imposes a form of discipline on women and defends his proposal on the grounds of the character of women's relation to men suggests that the reinforcement of gender differences would have been its likely effect. See Elisabeth Schüssler Fiorenza, *In Memory of Her: A Feminist Theological Reconstruction of Christian Origins* (New York: Crossroad, 1983), 230.

7. "No other distinction between man and man goes so deep as that in which the human male and the human female are so utterly different from each other" (*CD*, III/4, 118); cf. Hans Urs von Balthasar, *Dramatis Personae: Persons in Christ*, vol. 3 of *Theo-Drama: Theological Dramatic Theory*, trans. Graham Harrison [San Francisco: Ignatius, 1992], 285–88. See chapter 9 for further discussion of the theological significance of gender.

In practice, Ephesians 5 has served as a classic prooftext for the subordination of wives to husbands. Insofar as this subordination is explicitly based on the church's subordination to Christ (Eph. 5:23–24), the argument implicitly correlates human difference with the occupation of fixed social roles in which some are necessarily and inherently subordinate to others.[8] It is therefore hardly surprising that Ephesians lists a whole series of hierarchically ordered relationships, of which marriage is merely the first. The logic of the argument is clear: if the relationship between Christ and the church is the prototype for all relationships between different sorts of people, then all such relationships will be characterized by the same relationship of super- and subordination that marks this primary relationship.

One strategy for challenging this correlation of difference with hierarchy is to deny ultimate reality or permanence of sexual difference in Christ. Whatever the precise origins of the baptismal formula cited by Paul in Gal. 3:28, it is clear that some early Christians understood the statement that "in Christ...there is no longer male and female" to refer to the transcendence of sexual difference.[9] Whether or not such beliefs were widely held in any of the churches addressed by Paul, they certainly were current in some early Christian communities.[10] As already noted, Paul himself comes down against any such christological erasure of gender difference (1 Cor. 11:11). At the same time, his defense of this position in terms of the superordination of man as the "head" of woman (1 Cor. 11:3; cf. v. 7) raises the question of whether the only alternative to the erasure of difference is its interpretation as the manifestation of ascending degrees of ontological preeminence.

Any third possibility must be able to make sense of the apparent contradictions between the positions outlined in Ephesians 5 and Galatians 3. The classic strategy for reconciling such apparent contradictions in scripture is to interpret more obscure passages in light of clearer ones. Such a strategy might appear to give the edge to

8. Feminist theologians have argued that this correlation of gender difference with hierarchy invariably leads to other manifestations of difference being interpreted hierarchically. See, for example, Elisabeth Schüssler Fiorenza, *But She Said: Feminist Practices of Biblical Interpretation* (Boston: Beacon, 1992), 115–17.
9. See Rosemary Radford Ruether, *Women and Redemption: A Theological History* (London: SCM, 1998), 23–24.
10. See, e.g., *Gospel of Thomas* 114 and *Gospel of Philip* 68, in *The Nag Hammadi Library in English*, ed. James H. Robinson (San Francisco: Harper & Row, 1977), 130, 141.

Ephesians, which seems much less ambiguous in its practical directives than the more debatable implications of a verse like Gal. 3:28. Before hastening to this conclusion, however, it is worth pausing to consider whether grammar is always the best measure of clarity in scripture. If it were, the devil's citation of scripture in Matt. 4:6 would be unimpeachable, and it would be rather difficult to make sense of the nearly universal Christian condemnation of slavery in light of the various biblical injunctions urging (Christian) slaves to obey their masters. These points suggest that the broadly canonical criterion of consistency with the good news of Jesus Christ is a more plausible measure of clarity than grammatical specificity.

Using this criterion in defending a nonhierarchical view of gender relations frees one from the need to develop tortuous arguments defending every biblical text from the charge of patriarchalism. The advantages of being released from this obligation are clear, given that a considerable number of passages (e.g., Col. 3:18; 1 Tim. 2:11–15; 1 Pet. 3:1–2, not to mention Old Testament texts like Gen. 3:16) explicitly subordinate women to men in a way that opens the door to a more general hierarchicalization of the relations between persons. The point is simply that as Christians we do not read these texts in isolation, but in the larger canonical context within which they are situated. The question is therefore whether this wider context supports or undermines the correlation of difference with relationships of super- and subordination.

Ephesians 5:21–33 provides an ideal test case for applying this canonical criterion to the issue of human difference. If these verses are not the most aggressively patriarchal in scripture, they nevertheless provide the most developed theological argument in the New Testament for Christian androcentrism. Karl Barth, for example, contended that this passage provides an "exegetical norm" for the interpretation of human existence in general and the relationship between men and women in particular.[11] And though Barth claimed that the pattern of subordination outlined in these verses has "nothing really to do with patriarchalism," the fact that he felt it necessary to defend the writer

---

11. Barth, *CD*, III/2, 313; cf. *CD*, III/4, 150–72, and von Balthasar, *Persons in Christ*, 288–92.

from the charge of having betrayed the egalitarianism of texts like Gal. 3:28 is indicative of the difficulties posed by this text.[12]

These difficulties are not addressed by viewing Ephesians 5 either as a corruption of some more pristine form of the gospel or as a comparatively enlightened modification of Greco-Roman patriarchy.[13] The first option does not take seriously the text's canonical status, while the second fails to reckon with the devastating impact it has had on the lives of women in the church. Neither faces the central canonical question this text poses: granted its early and consistent reception by the church as canonical, how does this text bear witness to the gospel? Only once this question has been answered is it possible to go on to inquire about the implications of this passage for Christian thinking about human personhood.

As a first step toward such an answer, it is necessary to locate this passage both within Ephesians itself and within the New Testament as a whole. With respect to the first issue, there is a broad consensus that Ephesians falls into two main sections: three chapters of doxology (chs. 1–3), which provide the theological warrant for three chapters of instruction (chs. 4–6). The concluding verses of chapter 5 thus fall in the second section, and stand at the head of a table of household duties (*Haustafel*) that extends to 6:9.[14]

Just as significant for the present argument, however, is the canonical location of the verses in question. Here it may be observed that Eph. 5:21–33 is a pivotal passage in the description of the relations between women and men within the New Testament. Significantly, it falls (both canonically and, by critical consensus, historically) between two other benchmark texts, 1 Cor. 11:2–16 and 1 Tim. 2:9–15. Yet in distinction from both these other texts, only Ephesians offers a fully developed argument for gender hierarchy in consistently christological terms.[15]

---

12. See Barth, *CD*, III/2, 314.

13. Luise Schottroff points out that the differences between Ephesians 5 and non-Christian apologies for patriarchy are not especially pronounced (*Lydia's Impatient Sisters: A Feminist Social History of Early Christianity* [Louisville: Westminster John Knox, 1995], 22–33).

14. Though there is a good deal of scholarly disagreement about possible origins in Greco-Roman and/or Jewish culture of the *Haustafel*, it is widely recognized as a distinct literary form that reappears in Col. 3:18–4:1 and 1 Pet. 2:13–3:7, with partial parallels in Titus 2:1–10 and 1 Timothy passim.

15. Paul also justifies his recommendations in 1 Cor. 11:2–10 christologically, but the

This last point is theologically crucial in light of the claim that Jesus is the sole determinant of our identities as persons. If Jesus is the criterion for Christian talk about personhood, it follows that no argument for hierarchy among persons can be theologically binding unless it has a clear christological warrant. The significance of the argument presented in Eph. 5:21–33 cannot, therefore, be underestimated. Though it ostensibly pertains solely to the relationship between husbands and wives, it provides a framework to which all defenses of human hierarchy must ultimately appeal if they are to be theologically persuasive.[16]

To argue that Eph. 5:21–33 plays this canonically pivotal role is not to deny that the differences between it and 1 Cor. 11:2–16 and 1 Tim. 2:9–15 are considerable. For example, both 1 Corinthians and 1 Timothy speak of men and women in general, while Ephesians speaks of husbands and wives in particular. Likewise, where 1 Corinthians and 1 Timothy focus on personal deportment in the context of the public witness of the church, Ephesians seems to have domestic relations in mind. Nevertheless, canonical ordering and the actual use of these texts in the church suggest a cumulative argument in which Ephesians 5 provides a more explicit theological grounding for a pattern of gender hierarchy that appears to be defended in 1 Corinthians 11, while the effect of 1 Timothy 2 is to consolidate and intensify this hierarchalization of gender relations.

Historical-critical research has thrown considerable light on circumstances that contributed to the "patriarchalization" of the early Christian movement, including such factors as pressure to conform to wider social norms and reaction against movements judged to be heterodox. Such accounts, however, do not address the theological problem of understanding how the model of relationships between men and women prescribed in these biblical texts squares with other, antihierarchical strands of the New Testament witness. Is it possible to make sense of the language in the latter part of Ephesians 5 in light of these other textual voices?

---

subordinationist thrust of this argument is undercut by his insistence that man and woman should not be viewed in isolation from one another "in the Lord" (v. 11).

16. This perspective is shared by Barth, *CD*, III/2, 313.

A READING OF EPHESIANS 5:21–33

The argument developed in the latter part of Ephesians 5 takes for granted that Jesus' ministry lays the foundation for a specifically Christian understanding of interpersonal relationships. While we have no way of knowing exactly what the writer of Ephesians knew of that ministry, the fact that the church has given canonical status to the depiction of Jesus presented in the four Gospels gives these texts authoritative status for a specifically theological interpretation of Ephesians 5. A defining characteristic of the canonical evangelists' depiction of Jesus is the latter's explicit rejection of hierarchy among his followers. In the Synoptics this challenge is epitomized in Jesus' insistence that his disciples are not to model their understanding of authority on that of the authorities in the world at large. Instead, they are to show greatness by service and, indeed, by assuming the role of the slave (Matt. 20:24–28; Mark 10:41–45; Luke 22:24–27; cf. Matt. 23:8–12). This same theme is picked up in the Johannine report of how Jesus washed his disciples' feet at the last supper (John 13:3–17).

That this common witness of the evangelists is broadly consistent with the Christology of Ephesians is clear from the fact that the injunction "Be subject to one another in the fear of Christ" (Eph. 5:21) serves as the occasion for the discussion of the specific duties of husbands and wives.[17] The problem is that this summons to *mutual* subordination in Christ appears to be inconsistent with the ensuing argument for the *unilateral* subordination of wives to husbands.[18]

As a first step to exploring this tension (and its implications for theological anthropology), it is important to note that Eph. 5:21–33 presupposes that human persons are genuinely different from one another. The distinction between man and woman in particular is not accidental or ephemeral, but a constitutive feature of human personhood. This point is, moreover, the source of a real theological difficulty: for inasmuch as human persons are genuinely different

---

17. While the verb used in Ephesians to describe mutual subordination (*hypotassō*) is not the same used in the Gospels to commend mutual service, its use in Ephesians clearly parallels Jesus' command to serve (*diakoneō*) one another in Matt. 20:28 and pars.

18. Francis Watson also cites this apparent contradiction as evidence that Ephesians 5 suggests "if not the abolition, at least the *deconstruction* of patriarchal marriage," though his understanding of how this deconstruction is accomplished is different from mine (*Agape, Eros, Gender: Towards a Pauline Sexual Ethic* [Cambridge: Cambridge University Press, 1999], 234).

from one another, they are not interchangeable in a way that would make the content of mutual subordination identical for all people in every situation. All Christians simply cannot be subordinate to each other in the same way at the same time. How, then, is the command to mutual subordination to be lived out concretely? Within this context, the whole of Eph. 5:22–6:9 is plausibly interpreted as an attempt to make theological sense of the differences between persons. These differences are interpreted as corresponding to different roles within an established series of hierarchies in which both the superordinate and the subordinate member have definite responsibilities.[19] In all three categories of relationship mentioned in Ephesians 5–6 (husbands and wives, parents and children, masters and slaves), the injunction to subordination (or obedience) is applied unilaterally. Restricting our attention to 5:22–33, we see that wives are instructed to be subject to their husbands, but husbands are not enjoined to be subject to their wives. This imbalance is justified on the grounds that the relationship between husbands and wives is based on that between Christ and the church (vv. 23–24, 32). Thus, wives are to be subject to their husbands as "to the Lord," and husbands are to love their wives "as Christ loved the church and gave himself up for her" (v. 25).

The argument is thus set up in such a way that any affirmation of equality between husband and wife appears to challenge Christ's status as "head" of the church, while confession of the latter appears to imply the unilateral subordination of one spouse to the other. Yet the shape of the text is such that the argument is not quite as seamless as this summary might suggest, because the exhortation to mutual subordination, upon which the particular subordination of wife to husband depends, is itself the terminus of a series of commands that depend grammatically upon an initial imperative in v. 18.[20] The full period

19. See Barth, *CD*, III/2, 313; cf. Markus Barth, *Ephesians: Introduction, Translation, and Commentary*, vol. 2 (Garden City, N.Y.: Doubleday, 1974), 609.

20. There is textual evidence for the presence of a finite form of *hypotassō* in v. 22 in Codices Sinaiticus and Alexandrinus, as well as in the Byzantine textual tradition; but the absence of any such form from the oldest extant MS (P. Chester Beatty II, which is followed by Codex Vaticanus) combines with the principle of *lectio difficilior potior* to support the judgment that these forms represent later additions. Watson suggests that the added verbs may reflect assimilation to Col. 3:18 and 1 Cor. 14:34 (*Agape, Eros, Gender*, 222 n. 2).

governed by this imperative runs through v. 23, and can be translated as follows:

> Do not be drunk with wine (which is dissipation), but be filled with the Spirit, speaking to one another in psalms and hymns and spiritual songs, singing and praising in your heart to the Lord, giving thanks everywhere for everything in the name of our Lord Jesus Christ to [our] God and Father, being subordinate to each other in fear of Christ—wives to their own husbands as to the Lord, because the husband is the head of his wife as Christ is the head of the church (he is the savior of the body).

The thought concludes in v. 24: "But as the church is subject to Christ, so also wives ought to be, in everything, to their husbands."

Subordination is thus characterized initially as a feature of life in the Spirit that is parallel to exhortation, singing, and giving thanks. Insofar as the application of these other injunctions is not limited to wives, the fact that wives in particular are singled out when it comes to subordination sits uneasily in the broader context of the passage.[21] The grammatical features of the text thus point to a degree of theological slippage that becomes more pronounced when the unilateral subordination of wives to husbands is grounded in the relationship between Christ and the church.

This slippage is visible in v. 24, where the adversative "but" (*alla*) accentuates the fact that the analogy posited in v. 23 between husband and wife on the one hand, and Christ and the church on the other, includes a profound disanalogy. In v. 23 Christ's status as "head of the church" is glossed as a matter of his being its savior; yet attention to the broader canonical witness (with reference to texts like John 11:26 and Acts 4:12) suggests that the same interpretation cannot apply to the husband's status as "head" of his wife.[22] By implicitly distinguishing a wife's subordination to her husband from the church's subordination

---

21. While commentators agree that the introduction of the *Haustafel* constitutes a thematic shift in the letter, they disagree over whether v. 21 is to be grouped with vv. 18–20 or with vv. 22–32. Ernest Best presents a good summary of the relevant arguments (*A Critical and Exegetical Commentary on Ephesians* [Edinburgh: Clark, 1998], 516). My point in omitting a paragraph break before or after v. 21 is not to deny a shift in focus, but merely to point out that, grammatically speaking, it is not as distinct as most translators and commentators suggest.

22. See Markus Barth, *Ephesians*, 615; cf. Karl Barth, *CD*, III/2, 315.

to Christ as savior, v. 24 acknowledges that the wife's subordination is not a function of the husband being the wife's savior. But insofar as Christ's status as savior appears to be the primary reason for his being described as "head," this disanalogy leaves open the question of what the theological grounds are for describing the husband as his wife's "head."

This question might be less troublesome if the command for wives to be subordinate to their husbands were balanced by a command for husbands to be subordinate to their wives, in accordance with the key note of mutuality struck in v. 21 (cf. 1 Cor. 7:3–4). Instead, husbands are directed to

> *love* their wives as Christ loved the church and gave himself up for it, so that he might cleanse it by a washing of water in the Word, and thereby sanctify it, so that he might establish it for himself as a worthy church, not having spot or blemish or any such thing, but so that it might be holy and blameless. (vv. 25–27)

Once again, the writer treats the relationship between husband and wife in parallel with that of Christ and the church, but now from the husband's perspective. The relationship between these verses and those immediately preceding imply that "loving" is to be distinguished from "being subordinate to" as the activity more appropriate to the superordinate marriage partner. So the husband is to love his wife as Christ loved the church—a love that entails the willingness to give himself up for the sake of the beloved.

In assessing the merits of this argument, it is worth noting that the command to love is no more restricted by Jesus to any one portion of the church than are his injunctions to mutual service (John 15:12, 17; cf. 1 John 3:11, 23; 4:7, 19). The parallel is further weakened by the author's statement that Christ's act of self-giving had as its aim the church's sanctification, since it seems doubtful that a husband can be said to sanctify his wife any more than he can be said to save her.[23] The writer seemingly concedes this point when in v. 28 he drops the issue of sanctification and instead urges husbands to love their wives

---

23. Interestingly, when in 1 Cor. 7:14–16 Paul does speak of salvation and sanctification in connection with marriage, it is in explicitly reciprocal terms.

"as their own bodies" (vv. 28–29). And yet it is unclear that this line of reasoning is any more successful in sustaining gender hierarchy, since the writer immediately adds that "we are *all* members of [Christ's] body" (v. 30; cf. 1:22–23; 2:16; 4:12).

If women and men are equally members of Christ's body, then men would seem no more suited to giving themselves up for women than women for men. Indeed, the fact that all are members of the one body of Christ suggests that the practice of "giving oneself up for another" is inseparable from that of "being subject to one another," in accordance with Christ's own declaration that he came "to serve *and* to give his life" (Matt. 20:28; Mark 10:45). It would therefore seem that the practices of subordination and love are binding on all Christians in such a way that would disallow their distribution among different groups in accordance with a fixed hierarchy of relationships based on gender (or, by extension, on age, race, or class).

The final verses of Ephesians 5 bring the issue of the relationship between husbands and wives on the one hand, and Christ and the church on the other, to a head. The author relates the claim that all believers are members of Christ's body to the words of Gen. 2:24: "For this reason a man will leave his father and mother and be joined to his wife, and the two will become one flesh" (v. 31). The marital relation is then referred back to Christ: "This is a great mystery, and I am applying it to Christ and the church" (v. 32). Based on the argument to this point, however, the degree to which this parallel can be used to justify hierarchy is doubtful, insofar as those aspects of Christ's relationship to the church that clearly involve super- and subordination do *not* apply to the relationship between husband and wife. It is thus worthy of note that the writer again resorts to an adversative when he returns to the subject of husbands and wives: "But (*plēn*) let each one of you love his own wife as he loves himself, and let the wife fear her husband" (v. 33; cf. v. 24).

This rather abrupt return to the theme of wifely subordination highlights a defining feature of the passage as a whole. For while the ostensible subject matter of vv. 21–33 is the relationship between husband and wife, the effect of the argument is to focus the reader's attention on the person of Christ. In one respect this is exactly what the writer intends, since he construes Christ's relationship to the church as the basis for gender hierarchy within marriage. Yet this strategy also raises problems, for it is precisely at those points where the hierarchical character of the relationship between Christ and the church is clearest (viz., respecting Christ's status as the church's savior and sanctifier) that the parallel with husband and wife breaks down. Correlatively, when the soteriological effect of Christ's relationship to the church is held to one side, the concrete shape of his ministry seems to provide very doubtful support for any generalized subordination of one category of persons to another.

ANTHROPOLOGICAL IMPLICATIONS

If the foregoing analysis is at all on target, Ephesians 5 does not present theologically sound advice on the proper form of the relationship between husbands and wives.[24] Yet in the attempt to ground this particular human relationship—and, by extension, all others—in the sovereignty of Christ, the writer forces us to reflect on the character of that rule. As already noted, Jesus himself both warned his followers against establishing hierarchical relationships and characterized his own role as that of a servant. But as prominent as Jesus' critique of hierarchy within the Gospels may be, there are also plenty of instances where he does assume a starkly hierarchical, authoritarian tone (see, e.g., Matt. 5:22, 28, 32, 34; 10:32–38; Luke 14:25–27; John 10:26–30). Granted (as the writer of Ephesians 5 implicitly concedes) that no Christian can arrogate the office of Christ, it remains possible that in any given situation someone may speak with Christ's authority, such that a failure to heed may be counted worthy of judgment (see, e.g., Luke 10:8–12; Gal. 1:8–9). It is therefore not enough simply to point out the tensions between Ephesians 5 and seemingly more egalitarian elements of Jesus' teaching; it is also necessary to explain how rejection of the unilateral subordination of one class of persons to another is compatible with the belief that Jesus' sovereignty can legitimately take hierarchical form in activities like reproof, correction, and instruction.

At this point, it is important to emphasize once again that Eph. 5:21–33 highlights a genuine theological problem, insofar as the command to "be subordinate to one another" is not patient of easy

---

24. See Best, *Ephesians*, 524–25.

application. It is logically impossible for everyone to be subordinate to everyone in the same way at the same time, and Jesus' own example suggests that there are times when it is imperative not to be subordinate, but to claim authority over others. In this respect, Ephesians 5 performs the invaluable service of forcing the church to ask what it means concretely to be subordinate "as to the Lord" (v. 22), and to love "as Christ loved the church" (v. 25), even if the patriarchal model proposed in vv. 21–33 is finally judged inconsistent with the overall character of the New Testament witness to the sovereignty of Jesus.

It is in this context that reference to the wider canonical framework within which Ephesians 5 falls proves helpful. In the Synoptic story of the Canaanite woman, for example, subordination to Christ (whom she addresses as "Lord" in both the Matthean and Markan versions of the story) entails a refusal to accept his assessment of the situation at hand (Matt. 15:21–28; Mark 7:24–30). Likewise, in washing his disciples' feet, Christ graphically displays his love as a matter of subordination to others (John 13:13–14). Both cases make it clear that one's calling as a person in Christ is not reducible to a pattern of behavior determined for all time by reference to one's position within a fixed hierarchy.

This is not to say that hierarchy has no place in interhuman relationships. That Christians have a responsibility to be subject to the social and political institutions of the non-Christian world around them is widely attested within the New Testament (see, e.g., Matt. 17:24–27; Rom. 13:1; 1 Pet. 2:13–17), but such responsibility is provisional (see, e.g., Matt. 8:21–22 and par.; Matt. 10:37 and par.; 1 Cor. 7:29–31). The existing order is not a source of salvation and, indeed, is perfectly capable of serving demonic powers (see, e.g., Revelation 13). Furthermore, Jesus' own example makes it clear that subordination is not a matter of kowtowing to the powers that be, but rather, entails seizing the initiative in a way that is likely to leave those in authority perplexed at best and enraged at worst. So in a contemporary context, genuine subordination to the marginalized members of society might require radical insubordination with respect to one's own government.

The provisional character of the Christian's worldly obligations within the New Testament appears to reflect the conviction that people's roles are defined not by the realm out of which they come, but by the demands of the realm to which they have been called. As Colin Gunton notes, while instances of super- and subordination should be expected within the church, they should be associated with inherently flexible and shifting patterns of relationship rather than with permanent roles.[25] Again, the case of the Canaanite woman is paradigmatic: her claims are initially rejected by Jesus on the basis of the ethnic identity that is hers by birth; but she is ultimately acknowledged by him on the basis of her faith in the power of the coming realm that Jesus represents. This does not mean that she ceases to be a Canaanite or a woman, but what it means for her to be a Canaanite woman can no longer be assessed exclusively on the basis of established ideas and practices; rather, it must be discerned in light of the reality that is to come.

Though this point can be discerned from the passages cited, it is precisely in Eph. 5:32 that its contours come into sharpest relief: "This [union of husband and wife] is a great mystery, and I am applying it to Christ and the church." While this representation of Christ as spouse may have been intended—and has, in any case, been widely interpreted—as a means of reenforcing a strictly hierarchical interpretation of personal difference, the fact that it makes Christ the measure of human relationships rather than the other way round makes it open to a far less conservative reading. The marriage bond was established with creation (Gen. 2:21–24), and it appears, in terms of all its specific features, to be a function of the gender identity given at the time of creation to individual human beings. Yet Eph. 5:32 teaches that this appearance is misleading. The significance of marriage does not derive from its roots in creation, but from the eschatological reality of Christ and the church. And precisely because the character of that reality is still being disclosed—and has been shown already to include such bizarre features as subordinates challenging their Lord and the Lord assuming the position of a slave—the roles of the participants cannot be determined in advance on the basis of their gender, race, or class. Rather, they must be discerned in an ongoing process of engagement with the good news of Jesus Christ.

In this way, the logic of affirming the church (and, by implication,

---

25. Colin E. Gunton, *The Promise of Trinitarian Theology* (Edinburgh: Clark, 1991), 80–81.

each of its members) as Christ's spouse, far from reenforcing established patterns of super- and subordination within society, actually
subjects them to a christological proviso. If the imagery of the body
suggests that the differences that mark the various members are ar-
ranged in a fixed, if mutually sustaining, order, that of Christ as spouse
serves as a reminder that this order is not revealed prior to the eschaton and certainly cannot be equated with the political status quo,
whether in the church or in society at large. While the differences
that mark the lives of persons are real (and, indeed, characteristic
of personhood conceived on a trinitarian model), the relationships
established by those differences are defined reciprocally in the process of living together as persons before Christ and not by reference
to some pattern capable of definition independently of interpersonal
encounter.[26]

The idea that the relationships between human persons should be
characterized by a reciprocity subject to a continual process of redef-
inition is perhaps nowhere either more evident or less controversial
than in an intergenerational context. However much we may be inclined to wince at the remarks pertaining to wives and husbands or
masters and slaves in the Ephesians *Haustafel*, it is my experience that
the writer's comments on parents and children tend not to generate
the same levels of discomfort: "Children, obey your parents in the
Lord, for this is right.... And parents, do not provoke your children
to anger, but bring them up in the discipline and instruction of the
Lord" (Eph. 6:1, 4). To be sure, at first glance these instructions seem
no less one-sided than those given to husbands and wives, and commentators have long recognized that the subordination of children to
parents (or, as the text literally puts it, to fathers) is structurally of a
piece with the patriarchal model according to which wives are subordinated to husbands and slaves to masters. The point is that placing
parents over children does not appear as inherently and unredeemably
oppressive as those other two relationships, given the expectation that
the character of the relationship between parent and child changes
with time.

---

26. Barth himself concedes that "what it means that man is the head of woman and not
vice versa... is more easily discovered, perceived, respected and valued in the encounter
between them than it is defined" (*CD* III/2, 287).

This experience is implicit in the writer's own reference to parents as those responsible for raising (*ektrephō*) children, which suggests that the relationship he describes is shaped by a particular task that has a clear beginning and a definite, if not necessarily well-defined, end. My relationship to my parents is not the same now as it was when I was ten, nor as it will be if at some point either of them should suffer a significant diminishment of their mental or physical abilities. Even if the category of obedience (which, following the hermeneutical lead of Eph. 6:2, is probably best interpreted in the sense of "showing honor") remains in some sense an enduring feature of a child's relationship to the parents, its specific content will change as and when the child passes into a state of maturity or the parents into a state of dependence. If something like this point is widely acknowledged even in non-Christian contexts, it acquires a sharper focus and clearer rationale when it is understood that the concrete form of the duties of parents and children are framed by the subjection of both groups to the evolving demands of their callings "in the Lord."

Consistent interpretation of the christological framework laid out in Ephesians 5 thus suggests that the relationships between persons in Christ are properly interpreted neither in terms of fixed hierarchies nor as a bland egalitarianism. They are better described as relationships of reciprocity in which the duties of each to the others are determined by the particular calling to which each has been summoned in Christ. Such duties will include periods of subordination that may (as in the case of children to parents or congregants to their bishop) be prolonged. At the same time, however, any given instance of subordination must be set in the wider context of one's calling as a person, and thus of one's responsibilities to other members of the body. It follows that no such instance can be viewed either as determinative or as exhaustive of one's identity as a person. On the contrary, any instance of subordination must be subject to constant review by all parties involved to ensure that it remains a manifestation and not a violation of personhood. Here most of all, all our ideas about what we are must take second place to the concrete demands of the one who makes us what we are.

– 8 –

Personal Difference
and Human Nature

Rowan Williams has suggested that there are certain contexts in which
the theologian's job is less speaking the truth than "the patient di-
agnosis of untruths, and the reminding of the community where its
attention belongs."[1] Beginning with the appropriation in chapter 2
of Mary Fulkerson's remark that the white male is not the measure
of human personhood, it has been the contention of this book that
theological anthropology is just such a context. To talk about persons
is always to draw a boundary that excludes. That kind of exclusion is
a necessary condition of talking at all, and it is therefore a risk Christians are unable to avoid so long as they maintain that speech, for
all its dangers, is preferable to silence. Given the enormous amount
of damage that has been inflicted as a result of overhasty attempts to
define personhood, however, a vivid sense of the provisionality of language is especially important in theological anthropology. This point
is nowhere more evident than in the attempt to describe what we
have in common as specifically *human* persons.

Poststructuralist analysis judges that conventional philosophical
and theological use of language presupposes that the categories under
which we group individuals (including species, race, gender, ethnicity, and sexual orientation) reflect some common, underlying essence.
Over against this more or less well-established "essentialism," feminist
thinkers in particular have advanced the "constructivist" thesis that
categories like "human," "woman," and the like are defined through
particular sets of socially encoded practices and are not simply neu-
tral descriptors of given realities. Establishing that such categories are

---

1. Rowan Williams, *On Christian Theology* (Oxford: Blackwell, 2000), 196.

socially rather than naturally determined provides a basis for challenging prevailing cultural assumptions, but it also raises the question of whether categories like gender signify anything more than a temporary configuration of human interests.

DIFFERENCE AND THE BOUNDARIES OF THE PERSONAL

Chapter 2 ended with a preliminary assertion and a problem: on the one hand, it was averred that human personhood is defined by difference rather than in terms of correspondence to some criteriological checklist; on the other, it was noted that this understanding of personhood was by itself incomplete and, indeed, somewhat disingenuous, since our use of the term "person" (at least within the material realm) is pretty much confined to human beings. In subsequent chapters a great deal of attention was given to the place of difference in shaping personal existence, with particular emphasis on the trinitarian matrix within which the term acquires its specifically theological sense. I suggested that "person" be defined in a purely ostensive manner, as referring to the persons of the Trinity. Since their personhood refers to what they do not have in common, it does not describe any shared ontological substratum.

If the theological use of the term "person" takes its bearings strictly from the internal life of the Trinity, then human beings cannot be considered persons in their own right. They become persons insofar as they are brought into the life of the Trinity through the Word taking human flesh in Jesus of Nazareth. The Word is in this way the common mode of human personhood: human beings are constituted persons because the Word addresses them, and they live as persons by affirming this Word as members of the body of Christ. The fact that all human personhood is mediated through the one Word of God, however, does not make the fact of differences any less crucial for human personhood than for that of the Trinity. As we have had occasion to note at several points in the preceding chapters, it is in their distinction from one another that human beings form one body in Christ.

Once this point is made, however, we are brought back to the obvious fact that we do not view every experience of difference as a mark of the personal. If our personhood is bound up with the Word having become a human being in Jesus Christ, then it must be possible to distinguish human beings from the many other creaturely forms that God did not assume. To proceed on these grounds to formulate criteria of the human, however, seems guaranteed to undercut the importance of difference in the quest for some identifiable "essence" that constitutes a common human nature more fundamental than "accidental" personal differences. This quest, in turn, calls forth once again the poststructuralist argument that such essentialist attempts at definitions of "the human" are invariably erected on the foundation of an excluded "other."

This situation raises obvious difficulties for a thoroughly trinitarian interpretation of human personhood, not only because the church has so often been implicated in the practices of exclusion and homogenization to which poststructuralists have drawn our attention, but also because the basic vocabulary of trinitarian doctrine is shot through with the very kinds of terms (like "person," "essence," and "nature") whose coherence poststructuralist analysis calls into question. Though the second of these two points in particular might seem to render the present account of human personhood untenable, I contend that locating these seemingly problematic categories within a specifically trinitarian context allows difference to be honored without sacrificing a wider vision of the human. Before elaborating this claim, however, it will be useful to review briefly some of the ways in which difference is treated in the New Testament.

NEW TESTAMENT VIEWS OF DIFFERENCE

James's remarks on the subjection of all creatures to "human nature" (James 3:7), along with Jesus' matter-of-fact declarations that human beings are of greater worth than sparrows on the wing or lilies in the field, are indicative of the degree to which "humanity" forms part of the conceptual background of the New Testament. Notwithstanding the commitment to the idea of a common nature implicit in these and other passages, however, difference also receives its due. Whatever the details of the ethnic and ecclesiastical politics that surrounded the deliberations of the Jerusalem council recorded in Acts 15 (cf. Acts 16:1–4 and Gal. 2:1–5, 11–14), the upshot of its deliberations was an affirmation of difference. Luke's account works from the premise that in Christ, God's promises to Israel had been fulfilled. That these promises included Gentiles was not in dispute (according to Luke, this point had been secured already by Peter's missionary work in Caesarea), but that they were to come to the Gentiles *as Gentiles*—that is, apart from a rejection of Gentile identity through (male) circumcision—remained a matter of debate.

By ruling that circumcision was not necessary, the council effectively decided that unity in Christ did not mean identity. Jews and Gentiles were implicitly acknowledged to have their own integrity and, correspondingly, their own place in salvation history. To be included as a person in God's realm, one had neither to become a Jew nor (a point the church very soon forgot) to cease being one. This principle finds more generalized expression in Paul's characterization of the church as Christ's body, in which all the members of the body are one body *in their multiplicity* (1 Cor. 12:12).

As we have already had occasion to note, however, Paul's use of this imagery is itself the source of concern insofar as the difference he celebrates seems to move quickly in the direction of just the kind of essentialism that critical theory has called into question. For example, it is in the chapter immediately before the 1 Cor. 12:12 reference to diversity that Paul correlates gender difference with discrete liturgical protocols for men and women (1 Cor. 11:2–16). As noted in the last chapter, the essentialism implicit in this argument was soon developed in explicitly hierarchical terms.[2]

Difference thus emerges as a problematic category within the New Testament corpus. On the one hand, it is affirmed over against attempts at homogenizing uniformity; on the other (especially in the later books of the canon), it tends to be "managed" in terms of a binary, hierarchical pattern of categorization (parent/child, slave/free, man/woman) in which each member is assigned a specific role with its own behavioral parameters.[3] Given the legacy of this witness for women in particular, feminist problematizing of the anthropological

---

2. See pp. 110–11.

3. An apparent exception to this line of development is the Jew/Greek distinction. In this case, however, the absence of any correlation between difference and particular social roles is paralleled by an erosion of the church's willingness to honor difference at all, as the estrangement of church and synagogue led to a thorough homogenization of Jewish converts to the norms of Gentile Christianity.

categories that Paul (and most Christians after him) have taken for granted seems amply justified.

Over against these concerns, however, there is the problem of how difference can be affirmed in the first place without reference to generic categories of some sort or other. In this context, it is useful to recall the variations in Jesus' behavior toward individuals marked as "different" within his context. As noted in chapter 7, there are certain forms of difference that he implicitly affirms, and others that he resists. To give an example, Jesus heals an unnamed woman of her hemorrhage (Matt. 9:18–22 and pars.), but he does not "heal" her of being a woman.

This distinction may appear trivial until it is remembered that some strands of early Christian thought apparently *did* conceive of being female as a state that called for healing.[4] Alternatively, it has not been uncommon for Christians to interpret physical affliction as having positive value in the education of the self, in a way that would appear to render its eradication morally problematic.[5] Had he followed this second line of thought, Jesus might have challenged the woman's infirmity being treated as a reason for her marginalization (which, in light of the legal precepts laid in Lev. 15:25, seems to be the main issue in the story) without actually curing it. As reported by the evangelists, however, Jesus' practice in this instance challenges both an unqualified endorsement of and the totalitarian attempt to eradicate all difference in favor of a uniform ideal.

Yet while Jesus' behavior implies that the categories of "hemorrhage" and "woman" have a certain narrative stability within the Gospel text, this in no way speaks against their being socially constructed. To the extent that Jesus functions as the touchstone for Christian understanding of what it means to be a person, the fact that he responds to these two constructions differently is something of which the theologian needs to take account. That Jesus seeks to eliminate "hemorrhage" (along with "leprosy," "blindness," "paralysis," "mental illness," "demon possession," and, of course, "sin") suggests that this form of difference is an impediment to fulfilling one's calling as a person. By contrast, the fact that Jesus does not treat "woman"

4. See chapter 7, n. 10.

5. See, e.g., John Hick, *Evil and the God of Love* (London: Macmillan 1985), 343: "A soft, unchallenging world would be inhabited by a soft, unchallenging race of men."

(or "Gentile" or "Samaritan") in the same way would seem to count as evidence that this form of difference is no such impediment and, indeed, may contribute positively to one's personal identity.

To be sure, things are somewhat more complicated than this simple contrast suggests. To stick with our biblical example, the fact of having had a hemorrhage remains part of the woman's history even after she is healed. In this sense, it, too, is a permanent feature of her identity. The fact remains, however, that it is such a feature as *something that has been overcome,* while her status as "woman" does not appear to be understood as something that either will or ought to be overcome in the same way. The question thus remains of how it is possible to make sense of this distinction between the passing and the permanent without lapsing into an essentialism that undermines the eschatological limits on our understanding of human personhood.

THE CONSTRUCTIVIST DILEMMA

A constructivist approach takes its bearings from the wish to honor difference over against the homogenizing tendencies of essentialist discourse. The problem is that it is only possible to honor difference by naming it, and every instance of naming takes place against the background of an excluded "other," thereby inscribing boundaries that establish an implicit essentialism. A thoroughgoing constructivism thus finds itself in the position of being able to say very little, with the ironic consequence that the very commitment to difference that grounds the constructivist project results in a certain paralysis when it comes to making normative claims.[6] In response to this dilemma, some feminist writers have proposed a "strategic essentialism," in which general categories are deployed as a provisional means of achieving emancipatory ends but are not understood to entail absolute ontological claims.[7]

6. See Serene Jones, "Women's Experience Between a Rock and a Hard Place," in *Horizons in Feminist Theology: Identity, Tradition, and Norms,* ed. Rebecca S. Chopp and Sheila Greeve Davaney (Minneapolis: Fortress, 1997), 33–53. See also John Webster, "Eschatology, Anthropology and Postmodernity," in *International Journal of Systematic Theology* 2, no. 1 (March 2000): 23–28.
7. For a theological assessment of strategic essentialism, see Serene Jones, *Feminist Theory and Christian Theology: Cartographies of Grace* (Minneapolis: Fortress, 2000), 42–48. Jones refers specifically to the work of Luce Irigaray (*An Ethics of Sexual Difference*

Though developed in a different intellectual context, the work of G. E. Moore suggests that the reasons for rejecting pure constructivism are not merely pragmatic. Writing in the early twentieth century, Moore sought to counter what might be viewed as the essentialist position that all relational properties are necessarily internal to (and thus constitutive of) the being of a thing.[8] This thesis entails the following: suppose a term T has a property p; if all relations are internal, then to deny p of a term would entail that said term is numerically different from T (where "numerically different" refers to its being a distinct individual other than T). Moore rejects this thesis, arguing that though a term that is not p *may* also not be T, the denial of p of a term does not logically entail that this term is other than T.

In other words, arguing the technical point that at least some relational properties of a term are external allows Moore to affirm that there is such a thing as contingent truth.[9] To return to our earlier example of the woman with the hemorrhage, while this character's being a woman is (at least on the basis of her treatment by Jesus) internal to her identity (such that to denigrate her womanhood would be to undermine her integrity as a human being), her having a hemorrhage is not. Indeed, Moore goes on to argue that to assume the opposite—that all relations are in fact internal—commits one to the untenable position that *any* true proposition necessarily entails *every* true proposition.[10] Be that as it may, so long as one agrees with Moore that at least some relational properties are genuinely contingent (i.e., are not logically entailed by others), it must be possible to distinguish a term from at least some of its relations.[11]

Considered thus far, Moore's defense of contingent truths is broadly supportive of constructivist insights. If Moore wishes to contest the

---

[Ithaca, N.Y.: Cornell University Press, 1993]), Diana Fus (*Essentially Speaking: Feminism, Nature and Difference* [New York: Routledge, 1989]), and Seyla Benhabib (*Situating the Self: Gender, Community and Postmodernism in Contemporary Ethics* [New York: Routledge, 1992]).

8. G. E. Moore, "External and Internal Relations," in *Philosophical Studies* (London: Kegan Paul, Trench, Trubner, 1922), 276–309. My attention was drawn to this text by Rowan Williams's essay "Trinity and Ontology" in *On Christian Theology*, 148–66.

9. Moore, "External and Internal Relations," 288.

10. See ibid., 300–301; cf. 308.

11. "It seems quite obvious that in the case of many relational properties which things have, the fact that they have them is *a mere matter of fact*: that the things in question *might* have existed without having them" (ibid., 289).

thesis that all relational properties are internal, however, he does not appear inclined to veer in the opposite direction of a thoroughgoing constructivism in which all relational properties are external to (and thus not constitutive of) a thing. On the contrary, while he rejects the idea that every property of a term is internal to it in a way that would subvert contingency, he is willing to concede that there must be some quality in *T* (e.g., a circulatory system) that is the basis for its having a particular contingent property *p* (a hemorrhage).[12]

Moore concludes that it is both possible and necessary to distinguish between a thing's contingent (external) and noncontingent (internal) properties. This conclusion, in turn, entails that there must be something about every term that constitutes it as a "thing" in the first place. In this way, Moore's argument supports the contention that meaningful talk of difference presupposes a genuine "over-againstness" that is possible only if a term can be distinguished from at least some of its relations.

Having moved this far in what might be construed as an essentialist direction, however, it is immediately necessary to pull back from any suggestion that the postulation of "things" underlying our talk about the world necessarily implies a one-to-one correspondence between those "things" and our words. The possibility of distinguishing a thing from its relations does not undermine the insights of structuralist and poststructuralist analyses of language. Even if (to resort again to our example) Jesus' practice suggests that "woman" may be intrinsic to a person's identity in a way that "hemorrhage" is not, that point does little to clarify what a "woman" is. Insofar as the identification of someone as "woman" is connected with the particular features of her history in a given social context, it is no less socially constructed than "hemorrhage." It is, in other words, only through its history that any "thing"—including the human subject—appears, even though there are good reasons for resisting the temptation to reduce the identity of the subject to her history.[13] Thus, while thoroughgoing constructivism is logically problematic, constructivists' attention to the ways in which

---

12. "In other words...the relational property *entails* some quality in the term, though no quality in the term *entails* the relational property" (ibid., 309).

13. "We cannot but treat [individuals] as the subjects of their distinct histories, even though [none] is real *apart* from those histories: there is no Lockean substrate to be excavated" (Williams, *On Christian Theology*, 151).

personal identity is socially defined and regulated does help to check the reduction of a subject's identity to any particular aspect of her history.

Rowan Williams has proposed that this situation argues for "a kind of 'negative metaphysics'" that specifies what we cannot do in talking about an irreducible human subject rather than what we can.[14] This negative theme is also visible in Mary Fulkerson's attempt to check theological essentialism by means of contingent and always provisional statements of what the *imago Dei* is not. Both positions would therefore seem to be consistent with an eschatological interpretation of human personhood as that which is disclosed in and through an individual's history without being identifiable with any particular aspect of that history.

The challenge to such an eschatological anthropology lies in maintaining the open-ended character of our specific identities as human persons without glossing over the particular manifestations of difference that may be constitutive of those identities. In other words, if human beings are not to be reduced to their histories, neither are their histories to be viewed as a random accumulation of transient features that fail to constitute an enduring and identifiable subject. If individual difference is to be affirmed in a meaningful way, it is important that the citizens of the heavenly Jerusalem be identifiable as Ruth, Mary, Peter, or Paul and, insofar as these individuals are shaped by the concrete particularity of their histories, as women and men, Jews and Gentiles, Asians and Africans. What is required is therefore an ontology capable of affirming difference as an integral feature of human life without presuming to essentialize such differences in a way that suggests that they exist independently of the histories that shape individual lives.

A TRINITARIAN INTERVENTION

In the fourteenth century, John Duns Scotus, dissatisfied with existing attempts to give difference its due, attempted to articulate an ontology capable of doing justice to uniqueness of the individual. Scotus followed the Aristotelian epistemology of the age in taking it as given

---

14. Ibid.

that we do not know a thing in its individuality, but only by reference to the properties it shares with other individuals having the same common nature. Nevertheless, for Scotus (who was enough of a realist to argue that concepts correspond to reality), the fact that we are able to distinguish a thing's nature from its individuality demands that some objective correlate—what Scotus termed *haecceitas*, or "thisness"—be postulated as the ontological basis for an individual thing's unrepeatable uniqueness.[15] Scotus himself specifically exempted the Trinity from his theory of individuation.[16] In making this exception, Scotus seemingly wanted to avoid suggesting that the distinction of the persons was a subsequent modification of some logically prior divine reality. As we have had occasion to note earlier, however, the defining characteristics of classical trinitarianism forestall any such misunderstanding. The possible subordination of the persons to their shared nature is effectively ruled out by the trinitarian principle that the "essential" attributes of the divine nature are not specifiable independently of the persons. Because the communion of the persons defines the content of the nature and its attributes, logical priority belongs to the particular and not the general.

As discussed in chapter 3, this insistence on the ontological priority of person over nature is a defining feature of classic trinitarian doctrine as formulated by the Cappadocians.[17] John Zizioulas has expressed this priority by speaking of the relations among the persons constituting the divine being.[18] Because God is Trinity—and thus primordially personal—God's identity is not determined or constrained by an ontologically prior essence; rather, the divine essence is the expression of the mutual coinherence (or perichoresis) of the persons, and thus a manifestation of divine freedom.

Interpreted in this way, the doctrine of the Trinity provides an ex-

---

15. For an excellent discussion of Scotus's views on individual difference, see "The Realism of Scotus" and "Scotus' Individuation Theory" in Allan B. Wolter, *The Philosophical Theology of John Duns Scotus*, ed. Marilyn McCord Adams (Ithaca, N.Y.: Cornell University Press, 1990), 42–53, 68–97.

16. John Duns Scotus, *Ordinatio*, §39, vol. 7 of *Ioannis Duns Scoti Opera Omnia* (Vatican City: Vatican Polyglot, 1973), 408; cited in Wolter, "Scotus' Individuation Theory," 94.

17. See pp. 32–35.

18. John D. Zizioulas, *Being as Communion: Studies in Personhood and the Church* (Crestwood, N.Y.: St. Vladimir's Seminary Press, 1985), 46.

ample of individuation that overcomes the tension between universal and particular that burdens Scotus's own presentation of nature and *haecceitas* as quasi-independent metaphysical principles. On the one hand, the three persons in their unrepeatable identities as persons are the concrete forms of individuating difference within the divine nature; on the other, it is precisely the communion of these persons that defines that nature as divine. Instead of standing over against difference, the concept of nature emerges within a trinitarian framework as an "essence" that is constituted only in and through difference.

ANTHROPOLOGICAL APPLICATION

To the extent that Christians understand human nature to be defined by the incarnation of one of the divine persons, the career of Jesus seems to provide reasonable grounds for positing an analogue in the creaturely sphere to the peculiar logical relationship between the divine nature, on the one hand, and the three divine persons, on the other. Viewed in this trinitarian perspective, humanity is not an independently existing reality that is subsequently given a personal content; rather, what it is to be human is defined by the life of the divine person who takes flesh in Jesus of Nazareth.[19] At the same time, the fact that it is precisely by living his own unrepeatable existence that Jesus was made a specifically *human* being like us "in every respect" (Heb. 2:17; cf. Gal. 4:4) suggests that "humanity" has its shape as a distinct mode of creaturely being in and through the diversity of all those who are claimed as persons by God in Christ. In other words, the fact that human beings have been elected in Jesus Christ to become sharers in the divine nature (2 Pet. 1:4) suggests that human nature is every bit as much defined by personal difference as the divine.

There are also, of course, crucial dissimilarities between the divine and the human spheres. For example, Gregory of Nazianzus notes that the Godhead is "a union of mind, and an identity of motion, and a convergence of its elements to unity... which is impossible to the created nature."[20] While God is three persons in one nature inherently

---

19. "The nature of the man Jesus alone is the key to the problem of human nature" (Barth, *CD*, III/2, 43; cf. 59).

20. Gregory of Nazianzus, *The Third Theological Oration*, in *Cyril of Jerusalem, Gregory*

and from all eternity, the single nature of "humanity" is revealed in time and only by virtue of God's gracious election and equally gracious guidance. This latter work, traditionally subdivided into the operations of preservation (*conservatio*), accompaniment (*concursus*), and direction (*gubernatio*), defines a narrative framework according to which the creature's identity, though given in and with creation, is fully established in its specificity only through a temporally extended process of what is traditionally termed "vocation."

This narrative structuring of identity is easiest to see in the case of individuals. For example, while the Miriam who dies at Kadesh is the same one who watched the pharaoh's daughter rescue the infant Moses, the particular content of her personhood is realized only through the cumulative interplay of character and circumstance that constitutes her life story. That this same process of narrative development is also a feature of "human nature" as a whole is clear from the fact that Paul can see Adam and Christ, for all their differences, as instantiations of the same humanity (see especially Romans 5; cf. Heb. 2:14), while at the same time allowing that the final form of the human is not yet fully visible (as is evident, for example, from the claim in 1 Cor. 15:44 that glorified humanity will exchange a physical body for a spiritual one).

Christians view the life of Jesus as the climax and key to the story of God's dealings with humankind (Eph. 1:9–10; Heb. 1:1–2). The centrality of Jesus' story does not, however, undermine the significance of the rest of humankind for determining the precise shape of human life with God. In the same way that Jesus' teaching is held to fulfill rather than abrogate the law (Matt. 5:17; Rom 3:31), so his story fulfills the human story as a whole by giving focus to other human stories and not by rendering them superfluous. If his story is decisive, it is not exclusive; indeed, Jesus himself declares that he will not be able to tell his own story without reference to those who have claimed him as part of theirs (see Matt. 10:32–33 and par.). Thus, if Jesus' identity as the Christ may be considered firmly established with his resurrection, what it means for him to be the Christ is still in the process of being revealed.[21]

Nazianzen, vol. 7 of *The Nicene and Post-Nicene Fathers*, 2nd series, ed. Philip Schaff and Henry Wace (Peabody, Mass.: Hendrickson, 1995 [1894]), 301.
21. "Christ is the 'last Adam'...as such he embodies mankind's whole dramatic sit-

When human nature is conceived as capable of definition without reference to the particular histories of its concrete instantiations, individual difference invariably appears as something of a modification of or even declension from the ideal. By positing personhood as ontologically prior to and not simply an "accidental" modification of nature, personal difference is secured as the framework within which all talk about a common nature must be set. Within such a perspective it remains possible to speak of individual identities being conditioned and shaped by this nature, but only so long as this nature is not regarded as definable apart from the still unfinished story of human life as it exists under the call of Jesus Christ.

The biblical story of the triune God's dealings with the world thus allows for talk of a common humanity as well as of individual human beings. But in distinction from classic essentialist views, the common nature (like each of its personal instantiations) needs to be interpreted as an eschatological reality that is not definable apart from reference to the totality of individual lives through which it appears. Insofar as these lives continue to proliferate in their unrepeatable and unrepeated diversity, the full content of this nature has yet to be disclosed. As the product of the interplay of characters and circumstances, nature is socially and linguistically constructed; but so long as this interplay is understood to take place under the providence of God, this process of construction need not be interpreted as arbitrary. Human nature is real; but its reality consists in its being the object of God's faithfulness through time and not in some ideal existence apart from time. It is a fact, but a fact of grace that is perceived in hope rather than sight.

As the concrete form of this divine faithfulness, the ministry of Jesus Christ can be viewed as the gracious temporal outworking of the fidelity that constitutes the divine persons as one God. In the same way that the divinity of each person of the Trinity honors the others in their distinctiveness, so humanity exists insofar as God in Christ makes space for human difference. Moreover, in the same way that the

---

uation in relationship to itself and to God. Not only, through his personal destiny (in Cross and Resurrection), does he become what he *is* and has always been; it is through the whole drama that he actually *becomes* the Omega...he always is" (Hans Urs von Balthasar, *Dramatis Personae: Persons in Christ*, vol. 3 of *Theo-Drama: Theological Dramatic Theory*, trans. Graham Harrison [San Francisco: Ignatius, 1992], 201–2).

three persons of the Trinity together define the divine attributes, so the divine faithfulness to "humanity" as a whole includes a fidelity to those varied forms of difference, which, insofar as they are characteristic of human life in both its individual and collective moments, are also part of the broader narrative of the divine economy and thus not subject to any full or final characterization so long as that narrative remains unfinished.

To give a concrete example to which reference has already been made in the last chapter, and that will be discussed at greater length in the next, the scriptural judgment that the creation of humankind as male and female is "very good" (Gen. 1:27, 31) seemingly gives Christians a stake in affirming that gender is a constitutive feature of what it means to be human. But the fact that the act of creation is the beginning of a longer narrative should render us doubtful of any interpretation of the distinction between male and female that implies its content can be determined in advance of the story's end. Rather, in the same way that the meaning of the constitutively human distinction of "embodiedness" is subject to modification in light of the hope of resurrection from the dead, so the significance of "gender" is open as long as the human narrative remains unfinished. What "woman" or "man" is, is still in the process of being worked out, even though the fact of gender difference as a constitutive feature of human being is established by its place in the biblical narrative.

At the same time, the assurance of God's faithfulness ought not to be taken to imply that every manifestation of differences is to be viewed in a positive light. As already noted, the story of Jesus suggests that in some cases God's faithfulness to humankind is shown by the elimination of difference. Jesus' practice clearly marks out some manifestations of difference—illness and sin being the most obvious—as incompatible with the integrity of human being, whether understood individually or collectively. Others, like ethnicity, appear more open to interpretation as forms of difference whereby human life may be enriched (see, e.g., Rev. 21:24–26).

In line with the idea that Jesus came so that human beings should "have life, and have it abundantly" (John 10:10), this resistance to certain forms of difference is probably best understood in light of the overriding theme of divine faithfulness. Within this perspective, difference is not a value in and of itself; it is valuable insofar as it is created by God, and thus included in the broad assessment of all that God has made as "very good." The difference represented by illness and sin are not part of this created order and need to be resisted because they threaten it by bringing the narrative to a closure that is both premature and permanent. In other words, the differences that Jesus resists are those that threaten to cut individuals off from the ensemble of relationships through which they find their identity as human beings and thereby contribute fully to the wider human story.

Needless to say, this observation is very far from giving us a readily applicable procedure for distinguishing those differences that are part of the richness of the human story and those that are not. The debate within the churches over the legitimacy of marriage between persons of the same sex is widely (and, I would argue, quite rightly) perceived to turn on this question, but shows no sign of moving toward resolution in the near future. Nor, as ongoing debates over women's ordination make clear, does general agreement on the created goodness of particular differences automatically generate consensus regarding the implications of such differences for Christian practice.

Perhaps the most pertinent point to be made here is that the debatability of these matters is part and parcel of the unfinished character of the human story spoken by God's Word. If the life and practice of Jesus gives some general guidelines, it is very far from providing a rigorous criteriology of the human. Nothing could be more misguided, however, than to suppose that this fact condemns us to inaction. In this context, it is worth considering the history of Christian reflection on slavery. Despite what might be taken as a few hopeful hints, the New Testament as a whole evinces no particular uneasiness about the practice of slaveholding, and certainly gives no suggestion that it should be actively resisted. Over time, however, the church has concluded (with a unanimity that is hard to find in virtually any other area of doctrine or ethics) that slavery is incompatible with human personhood. This judgment emerged from an uneven and contentious process of tracing out the implications of Jesus' practice, and if the time it required cautions against any pollyannaish optimism regarding the progress of Christian ethics, the fact that it emerged at all is a powerful sign that the narrative to which Christians are committed is both concrete enough to provide direction and open enough to allow for genuine growth and development.

THE CATEGORY OF HUMAN NATURE

Contemporary reflection on human being is defined by the problem of difference: on the one hand, there is a broad desire to affirm the irreducible character of difference in the face of all attempts at homogenization; on the other, the very capacity to affirm difference is bound up with the use of "essentializing" language. Long before the onset of modern critical theory, the Cappadocians struggled with the same dilemma and attempted to address it in specifically theological terms by affirming the priority of the three trinitarian persons over that of their common divine nature. Taking our lead from this trinitarian framework, the categories of person and nature can be viewed as related in an analogous way in the human sphere: insofar as God claims us as persons, what we are takes second place to who we are.

This conclusion allows difference to be affirmed without sacrificing the category of nature. This gain is an important one, because in light of the biblical narrative, Christians appear to have a stake in viewing the concept of the human as more than an arbitrary, if unavoidable, linguistic category. In Christ it may be affirmed as a particular mode of created being, which, as the object of divine care and faithfulness through time, has been claimed for a particular destiny. The human creature is distinguished from all others by the fact that it was the particular form of creaturely existence taken up by God in the person of Jesus of Nazareth, with the result that this creature's destiny is bound in a particular way to God's own.

And yet if we ask what defines a given creature as human, it turns out that this christological touchstone provides no clear lines of demarcation. We may feel quite comfortable in our capacity to distinguish a human being from a dog, a tree, or a stone, but insofar as human beings are distinguished from one another as persons whose individuality is not reducible to any common denominator, the identification of criteria of the human becomes extraordinarily hard. Rationality, capacity for relationship, and even (in light of Paul's claims in 1 Corinthians 15) the possession of a physical body turn out to be less-than-reliable measures of humanity, if for no other reason than that we can identify them only by abstraction from the myriad lives that define the human precisely in their irreducible particularity.

To be sure, our actions no less than our speech invariably betray the fact that we do not view every manifestation of difference as consistent with the human. Nor, in light of Jesus' own selective affirmation of difference, can this fact be viewed as objectionable in itself. Judgments about what it is to be human and what is inconsistent with humanity are implicit in our every word and act. In our ongoing attempts to fit our individual lives into the wider story of God's dealings with creation, we cannot help but bear witness to our beliefs about the final shape that story will have. Our goal should be not the impossible one of refusing to make such judgments, but of subjecting them to constant examination in light of the conviction that the nature that we possess—like that of the God who is its source—is shaped by and thus logically subsequent to the irreducible and unrepeatable diversity of the persons who share it, so that its precise form cannot be known fully so long as their lives go on. As Eugene Rogers puts it, "We must reconceptualize human nature not in terms of a predetermined end, immanent to a general human nature...but in terms of a God-determined end, or eschaton."[22]

Postmodernism is famous for deconstructing the idea of a stable subject no less than a stable nature. In the words of one writer, the fact that the subject is "fabricated from transecting acentric structures" means that it is "never centered in itself."[23] Such insights have led to a greater sensitivity across disciplines to the way in which our identities are constructed both individually and collectively. Christians should keep in mind, however, that the inability of human beings to guarantee or secure their identities is a defining feature of a faith that names human beings as creatures whose bondage to sin means that their lives have no fixed center and spiral toward their eventual dissolution. That this process is arrested and reversed is due not to any capacity of our own, but to the fact that God comes among us as one of us in the life, death, and resurrection of Jesus.

The claim that Jesus provides the reference point for Christian talk about the human does not change the fact that our lives are shaped by various combinations of genetic, cultural, political, economic, and linguistic vectors operating on and through us. The Word that becomes

---

22. Eugene F. Rogers Jr., *Sexuality and the Christian Body: Their Way into the Triune God* (Oxford: Blackwell, 1999), 264.
23. Charles Taylor, *Erring: A Postmodern A/theology* (Chicago: University of Chicago Press, 1984), 139.

flesh does not simply trump other words in a way that renders the details of our histories irrelevant, but it does provide for these other words the context within which they are to be interpreted, serving as a touchstone over against which they are revealed as created echoes of that Word or more or less explicit denials of it. Our identities, both individually and collectively, remain socially constructed; but in light of the gospel their construction needs to be understood as contextualized by the ongoing story of God's faithfulness to us. This story encloses us on all sides, shaping both the created nature in which we are called and the glorified existence that is prepared for us. The way in which a story that involves the radical transformation implicit in the move from creation to consummation can be viewed both as one and as our own is the subject of the final chapter.

- 9 -

Symptoms of Being Human

It has been the burden of the preceding chapters to chart a course between what I have taken to be two unacceptable alternatives in theological anthropology. The bulk of the argument has been directed against an anthropological essentialism that equates human personhood with the possession of more or less readily definable qualities. This approach, it was argued, paves the way both for the exclusion of certain people from consideration as persons and for the equally dangerous occlusion of human difference in the quest to secure personal identity by reference to some underlying sameness. Both consequences follow from a failure to honor the trinitarian context within which the term "person" acquires its specifically theological sense. As a result, essentialist anthropologies prove unable to secure what I take to be the central Christian conviction that human communion with God is a gift whose basic form is determined by the fact that God addresses us as persons in Jesus Christ.

The trinitarian matrix and christological form of human personhood means that its content is not specifiable in terms of a set of essential properties. In this respect, the theological anthropology proposed here has definite affinities with the constructivist emphasis of much contemporary critical theory. In the last chapter, however, I maintained that there are limits to the degree of convergence between a credible doctrine of the human person and a thoroughgoing constructivism. Pure constructivism ultimately leaves no way out of the dilemma with which I closed chapter 2: when personhood is viewed as absolutely independent of any common nature, it becomes very difficult to restrict its creaturely application to human beings, or, indeed, to give it any definite content at all. Moreover, inasmuch as the New Testament writers consistently interpret the election of human beings in Jesus Christ in terms of a general pattern of divine fidelity to this creature over time, there seems good reason not to reject the idea of a created human nature out of hand. In response to these considerations, I argued that a way forward might lie in following Eugene Rogers's suggestion that human nature be reconceived as an eschatological reality whose shape is presently visible only to divine and not to human eyes.

While this strategy averts the risk of an undiluted nominalism, however, it arguably remains afflicted by a lingering sense of arbitrariness. If one adopts the position that human nature is real but as yet unrealized, it remains unclear how far it is possible to speak of a peculiarly human form of existence in the here and now. If this existence is truly open-ended, how is one to know whether its final form bears any resemblance to life in the present? Perhaps the boundaries of the human are so flexible as to evacuate the term of meaningful content. Although the full, eschatological realization of human being as personal being may be expected to include surprises, however, the idea that the end-product might bear no specifiable ontological relation to the beginning is not consistent with the biblical theme of divine faithfulness, since faithfulness presupposes an identifiable and perduring object of fidelity. Some further reflection on human nature therefore seems in order.

KARL BARTH AND THE PHENOMENA OF THE HUMAN

Given his strong emphasis on the christological ground of human being, it should come as no surprise that a similar tension between constructivist and essentialist themes is a feature of Karl Barth's anthropology. Barth, too, begins his discussion of human being with repeated warnings against any approach that tries to define the human by reference to some catalogue of readily identifiable qualities or characteristics.[1] Among such qualities Barth lists all the usual suspects, including rationality, freedom, and self-transcendence. At best, he argues, all such candidates are merely "phenomena of the human, in which we can see symptoms of the human itself only when the latter

---

1. Barth, *CD*, III/2, 74.

is known to us, but which in and of themselves tell us nothing about real [humankind]."[2]

According to Barth, the problem with such "phenomena of the human" is not that they are simply false, but that they are relative and therefore incapable of giving us conclusive insight into human being. Insofar as they are identified by an act of autonomous self-understanding, they can be accorded definitive status only so long as we operate under what for Barth is the false assumption that humans are sufficiently autonomous to be capable of arriving at an objective view of their situation from within. The gospel shatters this delusion by reminding us that human beings are creatures, and that their Creator alone occupies the position from which an objective appraisal of their situation is possible. It follows that the only basis on which people can speak responsibly about the human is the act of divine solidarity with humankind made real in the life of Jesus of Nazareth. In Barth's own words,

> It is worth noting that the biblical message never addresses [humankind] on any other basis. It does not appeal to [human] rationality or responsibility or human dignity or intrinsic humanity. No other decisive presupposition is made except that every one who bears the name of [human] is to be addressed as such in the name of Jesus, and therefore... stands in an indisputable continuity with Him which is quite adequate as a point of contact.[3]

Allowing for terminological adjustments that follow from the fact that the term "person" is not a central category in Barth's anthropology, the upshot of his position for the present argument is that our personhood has its ground in the personhood of Jesus. When considering our status as persons, it is not our natural capacities, but the covenant of grace that God assumes with us in Jesus that counts.

Notwithstanding the frequency with which he insists on the importance of this christological framework, however, Barth is equally adamant that anthropology cannot be reduced to Christology. In part this simply reflects Jesus' distinctiveness as Savior: his life as the Word

---

2. Ibid., 122.
3. Ibid., 134.

incarnate is such that he is able to be "for" others in a way that the rest of humankind cannot. Just as important as the issue of Jesus' uniqueness, however, is a concern for the integrity of human nature. For as much as our election to be covenant partners of God must for Barth be regarded as a sheer act of grace that is not rooted in any worth of our own, neither can it be regarded as utterly adventitious. To do so would be to transform it from a gracious affirmation of our being to its cancellation or disruption:

> If God had given to [humankind] a nature neutral and opposed to [divine] grace and love and therefore to the fellow-humanity of Jesus, alien and antithetical from the very outset to covenant-partnership with [God], how would [God] have made [humankind] the being marked off for this partnership? A second creation would have been needed to make this partnership possible and actual. And this second creation . . . would have to be regarded as a contradiction of the first, materially altering and even replacing it. If we are to avoid this conclusion, there has to be a common factor, and therefore a correspondence and similarity, between the determination of [humankind] for this covenant-partnership and [human] creatureliness.[4]

So long as our election is understood as God's being genuinely for us, the "new creation" in Jesus Christ cannot be viewed as utterly discontinuous with the old. Because the flesh that God assumes in Christ is specifically human—so that it is the human creature and not stones of the ground that God wills to be children of Abraham (cf. Matt. 3:9; Luke 3:8)—it is necessary to affirm that the form of human beings' eschatological destiny is consistent with and appropriate to their created nature.

At this point Barth is quite happy to reintroduce the "phenomena of the human" he had earlier dismissed as anthropologically inconclusive as containing valid and important insights into the character of human being. To be sure, they can be reintroduced *only* at this point, once the fundamental determination of human being for God has been secured in Jesus Christ, because it is only when human beings have received from without definite knowledge of their status before God that they

---

4. Ibid., 224–25.

are able to determine which of the many "phenomena of the human" are genuine *symptoms* of human being. Even though such symptoms neither establish that nor explain why human beings have been elected for covenant partnership with God, they do tell us how this covenant partnership is lived out. In other words (to pick up a theme from earlier chapters), if none of these symptoms constitute the ground for our personhood, they do define its form. They establish that we are persons *as* human beings and not in spite of that fact.

Barth's own enumeration of the key symptoms of humanity is three-fold. Fundamental to human being in his view is life with other human beings. Compared to this "basic form" of humanity, all other phenomena "have no 'categorical' significance in the description of humanity, i.e., they tell us nothing about being in encounter and therefore about that which is properly and essentially human."[5] But even this most basic of symptoms does not stand alone. It is supplemented by extended reflection on the structure of the individual as an ordered unity of soul and body and as living in time.

Notwithstanding certain problematic features of Barth's analysis (most notoriously, his interpretation of male and female cohumanity as a hierarchical sequence of "A and B"[6]), it would be difficult to match its comprehensiveness or its penetration, and I will not venture to do so here. In what follows, I do no more than attempt to identify and briefly expound three symptoms of the human that seem to me suggested by the creation story in Genesis 1 and confirmed by the subsequent course of the biblical narrative. While these three have certain parallels with Barth's categories, they are presented from a rather different perspective that results in different patterns of emphasis. In any case, I do not claim that they are exhaustive. As signs of a condition, symptoms do not define what makes us human and therefore cannot be presumed to be present in every case. At most, they point to certain more or less typical structural features of our identities as specifically *human* persons. In this respect, they are a gesture in the direction of the "strategic essentialism" proposed by some feminists as a means of giving some normative content to our talk

5. Ibid., 249.
6. The "A and B" passage occurs in Barth, CD, III/4, 168–72, but the basic principle that man and woman are created in a relationship of super- and subordination is an integral part of the discussion in the second part-volume as well. See esp. CD, III/2, 296–316.

about human being without presuming final knowledge of the human.[7] While neither exhaustive nor definitive, such symptoms can provide a rough set of christologically normed guidelines for conceiving and promoting ecclesial practices conducive to human flourishing.

DOMINION

While a number of theologians follow Barth's lead in identifying encounter with other human beings as the fundamental symptom of the human, the theme of cohumanity is not the first to be struck in the biblical creation story. Instead, the first concrete description of human existence is God's declaration that the human creature is to have "dominion" over all creation: "over the fish of the sea, and over the birds of the air, and over the cattle, and over all the wild animals of the earth, and over every creeping thing that creeps upon the earth" (Gen. 1:26). This symptom tends not to be highlighted in contemporary theological discussions of human being. It seems too redolent of human arrogance and tyranny with respect to the natural world and is often seen as the ideological basis for the human exploitation of the environment that may have already done irreversible damage to the biosphere.[8] Whatever the uses to which this characterization of human being have been put, however, the first point that should be made with respect to any Christian interpretation of "dominion" is that it applies primarily to Jesus Christ. If in Genesis human beings are created to exercise dominion (*archetōsan* [LXX]) over the earth, they do so only through Christ, who is the source (*archē*) of all creaturely dominion (Col. 1:18).

This observation is crucial, because the dominion of Christ is not tyrannical, but self-giving (see, e.g., Matt. 20:28 and pars.). For Jesus to exercise dominion is to assume the role of a slave (John 13:13–14). Indeed, in the mind of at least one early Christian writer it is this way of exercising dominion that establishes Jesus' sovereignty (Phil.

---

7. See p. 131.
8. For the classic statement of this thesis, see Lyman White, "The Historical Roots of Our Ecological Crisis," in *Science* 155 (1967): 1203–7. For more extended and developed analyses, see H. Paul Santmire, *The Travail of Nature: The Ambiguous Ecological Promise of Christian Theology* (Philadelphia: Fortress, 1985), and Rosemary Radford Ruether, *Gaia and God: An Ecofeminist Theology of Earth Healing* (San Francisco: HarperSanFrancisco, 1994).

2:6–11). Moreover, this form of dominion reflects a wider pattern of divine sovereignty that is characterized throughout the acts of creation, preservation, and redemption by concern for the flourishing of that which is not divine.

In line with this pattern, it is important to note that the dominion mentioned in Genesis 1 refers quite clearly to a human obligation to the nonhuman. In other words, a defining characteristic of human existence is an orientation to other creatures who are as much esteemed by God as human beings are (Gen. 1:21, 25, 31; cf. vv. 29–30). Nor is this symptom of human being visible only in light of Christ, even if it is only in Christ that its full significance can be appreciated. As early as Genesis 2 the scope of human dominion is defined in such a way that it is inconsistent with any purely self-centered program of environmental exploitation. The first human being is placed in God's garden "to till it and keep it" (Gen. 2:15): if Adam is free (with one significant exception) to eat of the garden's fruit, he has this privilege as the one who is also charged with seeing to it that it continues to bear fruit.

Nor is the theme of care limited to the plant world. Adam's dominion also extends to the animals, which he is allowed to name (Gen. 2:19). That this privilege is a mark of power is clear, but there is no suggestion that it is a power to be exercised arbitrarily. Instead, it echoes God's earlier naming of the day, the night, the sky, and the sea in Genesis 1. In both cases the implication is that the names given are appropriate to the reality named, and that the creatures so named have an integrity that must be respected.[9] Even though none of the animals corresponds to Adam (any more than the day, night, or sky corresponds to God), human beings are not thereby authorized to regard them as beings with which they are concerned only incidentally. Insofar as the animals are to be nourished by the plants whose tending

---

9. Insofar as the names given the animals are appropriate to them, the act of naming implicitly refers back to the ultimate dominion of God. As Alexander Schmemann has observed, "The significant fact about life in the Garden is that man is to name things.... In the Bible a name ... reveals the very essence of a thing ... as God's gift.... To name a thing, in other terms, is to bless God for it and in it ... [so that the human being] stands in the center of the world and unifies it in his act of blessing God" (*For the Life of the World* [New York: National Student Christian Association, 1963], 4–5; cited in Eugene F. Rogers Jr., *Sexuality and the Christian Body: Their Way into the Triune God* [Oxford: Blackwell, 1999], 255).

is Adam's proper work, the fact that they are not bone of his bone or flesh of his flesh does not diminish his responsibility for them.

Adam may, of course, fail to honor his obligations to other creatures, in the same way that the faithless steward may set about abusing his fellow servants (Matt. 24:45–51). The present state of the environment is testimony to just such failure; but the neglect of this responsibility does not mean that it is taken away. Human beings cannot undo the relation to creation in which they have been set, and it should therefore come as no surprise that in attempting to ignore it we only succeed in undermining the conditions of our own creaturely existence. In this context, it may be pointed out that the symptom of dominion presupposes (and to that extent may be treated as including) those cognitive capacities that have so often been seen as the distinguishing features of human being.[10] The dominion we have is a function of our ability to analyze our situation over against our environment, and to manipulate the latter on an other than purely instinctual basis—a set of capacities we can no more escape than the position of responsibility for creation that they entail.[11]

If we were to stop our characterization of human dominion here, it would appear to be a fairly dreary business: a generalized obligation for the care of creation, which we ignore at our peril. To forestall any such conclusion, it is worth borrowing a page from Barth by emphasizing that the character of human dominion is completely misunderstood if it is not exercised gladly. The fact that human dominion is grounded in God's own is crucial here, for the fact that God regards creation as "very good" (Gen. 1:31) serves as a constant reminder that though the travails of creation may cause God to rage and weep in turn, God's rule over creation is rooted in a love that is freely assumed as a joy and not a burden. In giving human beings dominion, God invites them to share—as free, self-conscious, rational beings—in the

---

10. The symptom of dominion is thus roughly parallel to Barth's understanding of human being as the *soul* of her or his body in §47 of the *CD*.

11. Because we are talking only about symptoms, there is no need to maintain that *only* human beings are capable of rising above instinct. The fact that chimpanzees are able to use tools, and that this knowledge is evidently passed on "culturally" rather than genetically, means that at least one other species is capable of manipulating its environment in a "rational" way. The theological point is simply that, however it may stand with other creatures, human beings' natural endowments are linked to a particular role they have been assigned within the created order.

divine appreciation of creation's goodness. Where the joy inherent in this calling is denied, human dominion becomes inhuman, however conscientiously it may be pursued, because care that is not rooted in love ceases to be care and degenerates rapidly into acts of resentment and condescension that bear no resemblance to divine rule.

SEXUAL DIFFERENCE

As decisive and multifaceted as the fact of dominion is for human being, however, it is not exhaustive. Indeed, the naming of the animals in Genesis 2 that represents the first concrete instance of the human exercise of dominion also reveals that dominion is far from being exhaustive of human being. Adam is a single individual, but we discover that singleness is not a symptom of humanity, for God declares, "It is not good that the man should be alone" (Gen. 2:18). Of course, Adam is not alone. Even before the creation of the animals, Adam is in relation with God, but the isolation to which God objects is evidently not addressed either by the abiding presence of God or by the creation of other, nonhuman creatures. The divine protest against Adam's isolation makes it clear that human dominion is to be shared, but not with the God who is its source or with the animals who are its object.

According to God, what Adam requires is a particular kind of other: "a helper as his partner" (Gen. 2:18). The specific character of this other has already been disclosed in Genesis 1 as an otherness internal to human being itself. Humanity is neither solitary nor a series of roughly identical units; rather, when God goes about fulfilling the divine intention to make a creature having dominion over the rest of creation, the product is differentiated: "male and female [God] created them" (Gen. 1:27). The narrative in Genesis 2 expands upon the significance of this differentiation. Like the first human being, the animals are formed from the ground. But though they, too, are creatures, they are not human creatures. By contrast, the partner God intends for Adam is to be human, though not a carbon copy of the first human being. The woman God creates from Adam is different from man, but different in a specifically human way that allows Adam to declare, "This at last is bone of my bones and flesh of my flesh" (Gen.

2:23). Humanity is not reducible to a single type, but is characterized paradigmatically by the difference between male and female.[12]

Needless to say, sexual difference is not unique to human beings. The biblical writers are well aware of the fact that animals, too, are male and female (see, e.g., Gen. 6:19; 7:2–3). In this respect, sexual difference is one of a number of features (like the fact of being created from earthly elements) that human beings have in common with a multitude of other creatures. Yet in the creation story itself the distinction of male and female is mentioned only with respect to human beings. It seems reasonable to conclude that this characteristic is symptomatic of the human in a way that other features common to a broad range of animal species (e.g., vision, mobility, or nutrition by ingestion) are not.

As with dominion, the character of sexual difference is disclosed christologically. We have already had occasion to note that the writer of Ephesians refers the union of male and female to Christ and the church. This teaching implies that the significance of sexual difference is not reducible to the biological complementarity of the genders, however important that phenomenon may be in practice. If the union of male and female as one flesh is a symbol that refers to the nongenital (and still to be consummated) union of Christ and the church, then its significance cannot be regarded as fully known in the present. It points to the fact that human beings confront otherness not only when they look abroad to God or to the realm of nonhuman creatures, but also when they look among themselves. If, as the preceding chapters have argued, difference is decisive for understanding our existence as persons in Christ, the distinction of the sexes establishes that the relationship of mutual interdependence to which we are called as members of Christ's body is consistent with the creaturely identity we were given in the beginning.

If difference is a fundamental characteristic of human being, any attempt to be human (e.g., in the exercise of dominion) in solitude is a denial—and thus a fundamental misapprehension—of one's humanity. Because it is not good for a human being to be alone, they should not strive to be alone, in the sense of acting as though their humanity

---

12. This symptom thus reflects Barth's insistence on the essential form of humanity as cohumanity in §46 of CD.

were somehow self-contained. As Barth argued, to be human is to look the human other in the eye, to encounter the other in mutual speech and hearing, to render assistance to the other, and, most importantly, to perform all these acts with gladness.[13] In this way, he rightly stressed that life in communion with others is no more properly conceived as a burden on human existence than dominion is; rather, it is integral to what it means to be human. So Adam's response to the creation of the woman is one of joy in the face of a gift that calls forth a responsive act of self-giving that, far from diminishing his own identity, confirms it: "Therefore a man leaves his father and his mother and clings to his wife, and they become one flesh" (Gen. 2:24).

At the same time (and in line with the conclusions reached in chapter 7), the fact that the significance of sexual differentiation in creation is made clear only in light of the ministry of Jesus means that there is a significant gap between the basic affirmation that humanity is created male and female and the question of what exactly it means to be male and female. As Paul argues, the interdependence of male and female is not self-evident, but a truth that is known only "in the Lord" (1 Cor. 11:11). Inasmuch as our experience of God is constantly being enriched in the life of the community of faith, it seems prudent to be modest in our attempts to define sexual identity in terms of particular attributes or roles. If the theological significance of sexual differentiation refers most directly to the union of Christ with the church—a union in which individuals are called to myriad unsubstitutable roles within the one body—then the wisest course may be to conceive of sexual differentiation in terms of a broad spectrum of possible instantiations with respect to two foci instead of a binary opposition of two discrete types. Once such latitude is granted, it obviously becomes difficult to specify a particular form of relationship between such variably differentiated human beings as uniquely appropriate to human bodily existence as male and female, even if certain options (relationships based on the ownership of one human being by another, for example) may be ruled out. It should therefore come as no surprise to discover that throughout the history of the church, Christians have experimented with a variety of ways of living together

---

13. Barth, *CD*, III/2, 250–72.

as sexually differentiated beings.[14] The prototype here is Jesus himself, an unmarried man who practiced an itinerant ministry with a coterie of both male and female companions (Luke 8:1–2; cf. Mark 15:41). Thus, however much sexual difference is a sign of this orientation to the other, it cannot be taken as the last word on the subject. As Eugene Rogers puts it, "Male-female complementarity may be typical of co-humanity, but it need not be essential."[15] Our identities as male and female come into view only through a maze of densely netted biological, social, and psychological filters that undermine any immediate perception of the "natural" form or content of sexual difference, and thus of human being as such. While we see an important symptom of the human in our experience of male and female, we see no more than a symptom, and we therefore need to be careful not to presume to know more than we do regarding the state of which it is symptomatic. If even the apparently straightforward sexual complementarity of man and woman in marriage refers properly to the bond between Christ and the church, then the mystery of human otherness cannot be reduced to a fixed structure based on observable biological correspondence. What that final wedding will be like is simply beyond our present capacity to grasp; but in its light we do have a pledge that the differences we encounter in our experience of others here and now—differences that are by no means limited to those of sex or sexual orientation—are integral to our humanity rather than so many ways in which it is qualified.

FRUITFULNESS

The significance of human difference carries over to the final symptom of the human mentioned in Genesis 1. Having created the human creature, male and female, as the agents of divine dominion, God blesses them with the command to be fruitful, multiply, and fill the earth (Gen. 1:28). Here we have a symptom perhaps even more problematic at first glance than that of dominion. Is it responsible to speak

---

14. Linda Woodhead notes that "the variety of these communities is often obscured by our blanket use of the term 'monastic' to describe them" ("Sex in a Wider Context," in *Sex These Days: Essays on Theology, Sexuality and Society*, ed. Jon Davies and Gerard Loughlin [Sheffield: Sheffield Academic Press, 1997], 114).

15. Rogers, *Sexuality and the Christian Body*, 142; cf. 187–89.

of fruitfulness as a symptom of the human in a time when rapidly expanding population is placing untold strain on the carrying capacity of the biosphere? And does not an emphasis on procreation necessarily result in the exclusive valorization of heterosexual marriage that puts an end to all the careful warnings against overly narrow interpretations of sexual difference outlined in the previous section?

Both questions cry out for an answer, and a beginning may be made by remembering that here, too, we are speaking of a symptom and not a criterion of the human. It is emphatically not the case that a failure to produce children is a mark against one's humanity, as is clear, once again, when this symptom is interpreted within a christological framework. Jesus himself did not have children any more than he had a wife. He was, however, quite explicit both about welcoming children himself (Matt. 19:13–14) and about commending the practice to his disciples (Mark 9:36–37). In light of this example, the conclusion seems unavoidable that fruitfulness is less about procreation (which, like marriage, will cease with the eschaton) than about creating an environment in which children are welcomed.

Given that the destiny to which God summons us stands in essential continuity with our created form, it should come as no surprise that these specifically christological insights are fully consistent with broader human experience. The raising of children is never limited to the biological mother and father and (as the phenomenon of adoption richly demonstrates) does not even require them to be on the scene. Grandparents, uncles, aunts, cousins, older siblings, and even family friends may all play a more or less important role in nurturing younger life, as will neighbors, teachers, coaches, and other mentors. It follows that an individual's production of children has no direct bearing on her or his ability to exhibit this particular symptom of human being.[16]

At the same time, the focus on children reflects the fact that genuinely human existence requires openness to the intrusion of a third into the differentiation characteristic of human existence as male and female. In this respect, Eve's "I have produced a man with the help of the Lord" (Gen. 4:1) is analogous to Adam's earlier "This at last

---

16. Thus, the Ramsey Colloquium's claim that "only the heterosexual norm gives full expression to the commitment to time and history evident in having and caring for children" is simply untenable ("The Homosexual Movement: A Response by the Ramsey Colloquium," *First Things* 41 [March 1994]: 15–21).

is bone of my bones." Needless to say, the fact that children are also
male or female means that there is no question here of a third type of
humanity, as though the creation described in Genesis 1–2 were somehow incomplete. But children do represent a third, temporally indexed
form of human difference alongside the structural difference between
male and female.[17] It is a form of difference that marks all of our lives,
even after we grow to adulthood, and it has as a distinguishing feature the character of being both utterly one-sided (children cannot
survive without the care of adult human beings) and yet also mutually dependent (the human species as male and female cannot survive
without a commitment to children). Thus, while the relationship of
progeny to parent is lopsided during childhood, the future belongs to
the dependent partner.

There are, of course, other ways in which the fecundity of human
beings as male and female can take shape aside from childbearing and
childrearing. Among contemporary thinkers, Luce Irigaray has been
particularly insistent on broadening established views on the products
of sexual difference to include the full range of human cultural ar-
tifacts.[18] Yet at least one commentator has questioned whether this
laudable desire to avoid a purely procreative interpretation of sexual
difference (especially where women are concerned) does not tend toward an undesirably abstract and disembodied view of human being.[19]
Without denying that the products of human creativity may be en-
joyed for their own sake, an emphasis on the centrality of children has
the advantage of reminding us that the human significance of cultural
products lies finally in their capacity to promote and sustain an environment that is welcoming of new life. In short, rather than viewing
children as just one effect of human sexual difference, I am suggesting
that they occupy a central place in the human economy by virtue of

---

17. In this respect, the symptom of fruitfulness is roughly parallel with Barth's emphasis
on humanity's existence in time in §47 of *CD*.

18. "Sexual difference would constitute the horizon of worlds more fecund than any
known to date—at least in the West—and without reducing fecundity to the reproduction
of bodies and flesh. For loving partners this would be a fecundity of birth and regeneration,
but also the production of a new age of thought, art, poetry, and language" ("Sexual
Difference," in *An Ethics of Sexual Difference* [London: Athlone, 1993], 5; cf. *Sexes and
Genealogies* [New York: Columbia University Press, 1993], vi; cited in Tina Beattie, "Carnal
Love and Spiritual Imagination: Can Luce Irigaray and John Paul II Come Together?" in
Davies and Loughlin, eds., *Sex These Days*, 175, 181).

19. Beattie, "Carnal Love," 181–82.

the way in which they help to direct other forms of fruitfulness to the concrete particularity of new and different human bodies.

SYMPTOMS OF THE HUMAN AND THE CALL OF CHRIST

Drawing my candidates for symptoms of the human from the first chapter of Genesis brings the argument back to the vexing question of humanity's creation "in the image of God" with which this study began. I have maintained that the content of this image cannot be determined from Genesis 1, but is revealed only with the advent of Jesus Christ. In light of Jesus' coming, however, it is possible to go back to the creation story and interpret what is said there in light of the destiny to which Jesus calls us. Because the grace perfects rather than destroys our nature, the fact that we are created "in" the image that is Christ means that we have been made in such a way that the life to which we have been called with God must be regarded as an appropriate, if not strictly necessary, outcome to the human project. Thus, while the symptoms of the human found in Genesis 1 do not define the divine image, they are a means by which we may (albeit on a purely a posteriori basis) see something of its historical trajectory.

Nevertheless, the project of identifying symptoms of the human is a dangerous one because it runs the risk of slipping back down the road to essentialism. It is partly as a prophylactic against this risk that I have insisted on the term "symptom." Once one has independent knowledge of a condition on other grounds, it may be possible to see how its symptoms relate to it as appropriate (in the sense of materially consistent) corollaries; but symptoms can never be regarded either as necessary or infallible signs of a condition. Because a symptom is an expression of a condition and not its cause, one may have a condition without exhibiting any of its symptoms; likewise, the presence of a symptom does not demonstrate the presence of a particular condition.

Both these provisos apply to the "symptoms of the human" presented here. Sexual differentiation and concern for young are properties that extend to a host of other creatures besides human beings. If the first human pair is commanded, "Be fruitful and multiply," so are sea creatures (Gen. 1:22). And while angels are not mentioned in the creation narrative, they have been widely understood within the Christian tradition to exercise some sort of "dominion" in the created sphere (e.g., over nations or the motions of heavenly bodies). Nor should it be supposed that human beings necessarily exemplify these symptoms in a more exalted or exemplary manner than other creatures. For all we know, other creatures may in their sexuality, their fecundity, and in their own spheres of dominion glorify God every bit as much as (albeit differently than) human beings. In light of these considerations, humanity cannot be identified directly with the presence of these or any other of its possible symptoms.

Nor can the absence of any of these symptoms be viewed as a bar to the human. All human beings are not fruitful in the biological sense that is clearly the central thrust of the divine command in Genesis. Neither are all human beings endowed with the capacities of reason, reflection, and will that seem a necessary condition of the exercise of dominion over other creatures. Even the universality of human sexual differentiation is problematic, given the complex interactions of biology and society that shape our perceptions of what it means to be male or female. In light of these considerations, it cannot be emphasized strongly enough that no combination of symptoms can be assumed to provide a foolproof criteriology of the human.

Given these restrictions, it may seem doubtful that there is much point in identifying such symptoms at all. Yet they remain an important, if secondary, feature of any plausible theological anthropology, because without the possibility of identifying such symptoms, any account of human destiny with God risks losing its ground in the creature God created "in the beginning." If the final form of human being cannot be equated with its created state, neither can it be severed from it without undermining our confidence both that the being in question is genuinely human and that its ultimate glorification is a matter of divine faithfulness rather than demonic caprice.

It is therefore important that the symptoms of the human visible from the beginning correspond to the personal existence to which human beings have been called in Jesus Christ. The symptoms of dominion, sexuality, and fruitfulness are marked by such correspondence by virtue of the way in which they all point to the importance of difference in understanding the created nature as well as the final destiny of human beings. The human exercise of dominion requires attention to and respect for those creatures that are not human but that are also the object of divine concern. Human beings can and do fail to recognize this fact and treat other creatures with a disregard bordering on contempt, but however much they may scorn their responsibility for the rest of creation, it continues to mark their existence as a species, if only through the ravages of widespread environmental degradation that threatens human existence itself.

The symptoms connected with questions of gender and generation project the theme of difference within the human sphere itself. Here, too, it is possible for human beings to forget, misapprehend, or despise their being as male and female, or as "senior citizens" with responsibility for junior members of the race, but no such development can make human beings other than a creature marked by difference both in space and through time. Yet it would be equally reckless to conclude that these symptoms can be taken seriously only in the forms of heterosexual marriage and biological procreation. While both phenomena may quite properly be regarded as typical forms in which these symptoms present themselves, they cannot be regarded as the only forms capable of respecting the destiny to which the human creature has been called in Christ. Such an exclusive claim could be defended only on the false supposition that the protological and eschatological condition of human being are identical; but such a claim is inconsistent with the biblical emphasis on the difference between what we are now and what we will be.

This difference between the end and the beginning reflects the fact that symptoms of the human can be recognized as such only in light of the life of Christ, whose relation to us is decisive for understanding what our humanity is and means. In this light, we see that the relationship of marriage as established in creation has as its referent the eschatological union of Christ and the church. It is certainly not to be held in any less esteem for this reason (as the teachers denounced in 1 Tim. 4:1–5 seem to have suggested), but neither is it to be taken as the final word on the subject (as is clear from Jesus' remarks to the Saduccees in Matt. 22:29–30). In the same way, Jesus' reception of children obviously has nothing to do with his being a biological father. As Eugene Rogers has pointed out, the ancient practice of oblation is an important reminder that the church has not viewed the reception of children as bound by the physiology of human reproduction.[20] Indeed, within the New Testament itself, adoption rather than natural procreation is the decisive category for the constitution of human persons (see Rom. 8:23; Gal. 4:5). Children of God are not born, but instead must be reborn in a process that is a matter of Spirit rather than flesh, and of divine rather than human will (John 1:12–13; cf. 3:5–6).

This is not to suggest that the range of appropriate expressions of human difference in both its structural (male and female) and temporal (adults and children) form is infinite. It is simply to note that it cannot be defined by reference to a picture of human being taken as fixed and derived more or less explicitly from observations of biological function. Insofar as we believe that we have been created for a particular destiny as persons before God, and that this destiny is a gracious one, it follows that we are creatures for whom personhood is somehow appropriate. We may even gain some insight into the character of this appropriateness to the extent that we see our life as persons as a function of our having been addressed by the God whose own life is marked by that irreducible difference that the formulators of trinitarian doctrine named "persons." Seen in this context, the differences between human and nonhuman, between human beings as male and female, and between human generations all bespeak a creature for whom difference is already a feature of its own form and calling within the wider creation.

Within the context of creation alone, however, no firm conclusions can be drawn regarding the significance (or even the fundamental character) of these differences. It is conceivable that they might turn out (as some of the church fathers thought with respect to sexual difference in particular) to be a purely temporary expedient destined to pass away with the coming of God's realm. The conclusion that difference is truly symptomatic of human being can be drawn only on the basis of the subsequent fact of our being claimed as persons in Jesus Christ. As a particular human being whose address to us is the source and measure of all other human life, Jesus makes it clear that human difference cannot be contained (and thus finally ignored) by being organized into a fixed number of manageable categories. If our destiny

---

20. Rogers, *Sexuality and the Christian Body*, 260–65; cf. 208–10.

as human persons lies in the fact that God has encountered us in this
human being, then our personhood cannot be located within us, and
human difference cannot be interpreted as a veneer laid over some
identical substratum; rather, it is in our own particularity and thus
in our difference that we are addressed as persons. This conclusion
can be avoided only at the price of making our status as persons
conditional upon some factor alongside our gracious election by God
in Jesus Christ.

In this way, God's election becomes the touchstone against which
our understanding of the human is to be measured. We are the creatures whom God has from before all time intended to live as persons
in communion with God. The content of our identity as persons is not
something that can be determined from any segment of our creaturely
history taken by itself. What we are cannot simply be equated with
our original, created state (even assuming it were possible to come to
a clear understanding of what that state included); nor can it be identified with our calling, as though the latter bore no relation to (and
thus amounted to a denial of) our created being. Insofar as human
beings exist in time, theologically responsible talk about human nature cannot be abstracted from time's flow. What we are remains to
be seen, but it certainly includes what we have been. To paraphrase
Paul, it is those whom God created who have been called in Jesus
Christ, and those who have been called who are justified and glorified
(Rom. 8:30).

Thus, if our identity as human *persons* is caused exclusively by our
having been claimed as such by Jesus Christ, the fact that we are
specifically *human* persons is grounded in our having been created.
In creation we are marked not only by the fact of difference (a state
of affairs by no means unique to human being), but also by responsibility for it. In light of the call we receive to live as persons, this
demand for attention to difference becomes further defined as a ded-
ication to the other that cannot be limited on a priori grounds to the
symptomatic manifestations of heterosexual marriage and biological
procreation. Our relations with others will instead be defined by the
emerging patterns of relationship we enjoy with each other in Christ,
and be limited only (though quite definitely) by the commitment to
the integrity of the other that marks Jesus' own career. In any case,
our perception of what it means to be specifically human persons will

be determined by a process of discerning the body of Christ that must constantly be tested in light of the shifting patterns of relationship in which, through Christ, we find ourselves.

Having arrived at this point, it remains only to issue a final reminder that the life we have been given and to which we are called in Jesus Christ is not a possession that we can control or manipulate at will. As Albert Schweitzer long ago realized (albeit for very different reasons than those proposed here), neither Jesus nor the life he brings can be contained by our wishes:

> He comes to us as One unknown, without a name, as of old, by the lake-side, He came to those...who knew him not. He speaks to us the same word: "Follow thou me!" and sets us to the tasks which He has to fulfill for our time. He commands. And to those who obey Him, whether they be wise or simple, He will reveal Himself in the toils, the conflicts, the sufferings which they shall pass through in His fellowship, and, as an ineffable mystery they shall learn in their own experience Who He is.[21]

This book began with the assertion that the central question in theological anthropology is not what we are, but who makes us what we are. Schweitzer's words bring the problem full circle. For if it has been the contention of this book that Jesus is the one who makes us what we are; encountering Jesus forces us to reckon with the uncomfortable truth that his identity is no more reducible to a discrete list of characteristics than is our own. On the contrary, the ascended Christ constantly asserts himself over against our attempts to categorize him, whether or not we prove willing to recognize this fact.

If we are bound to acknowledge that Jesus comes upon us as one unknown, however, we also confess that he does not stay that way. Though he stubbornly resists our attempts at definition, he is not a blank slate; and the specificity of his story undermines our attempts to fill it in with whatever content we might wish. The Jesus who calls us now does not come in predictable form, but he is nevertheless the same one who called the disciples by the lakeside all those centuries ago. If his identity as risen Savior is manifest in freedom from the constraints

---

21. Albert Schweitzer, *The Quest of the Historical Jesus* (New York: Macmillan, 1956), 403.

of life in time and space, he realizes this freedom in faithfulness to those of us who are so constrained, ever claiming us from the forces within and without ourselves that threaten our place in the story of which he is the source and the ending. Through this faithfulness we know we are persons now; and if we do not yet know fully what that means, we know who gives it meaning, and that when in the fullness of time he comes again, we shall be like him, for we shall see him as he is.

Index

❖

fruitfulness, 155–59
Fulkerson, Mary M., 17–19,
    24–25, 126, 134

gender difference, 111–23,
    129–31, 139, 152–55
good Samaritan, 12, 76–81
Gregory of Nazianzus, 38, 136
Gunton, Colin E., 123

Haustafel, 114, 124
hierarchy, 101, 110–16, 120–22
Holy Spirit
    as mode of Christ's presence,
        84–89, 93, 98–100
    role in constituting human
        persons, 52–54, 59, 72, 101
    role in constituting the
        Trinity, 71
homogenization, 7, 24, 28, 83,
    107
homoousios, 32, 38
human, the
    phenomena of, 145–48
    symptoms of, 13, 148–62
hypostasis, 33, 39–41, 43, 50
hypostatic union, 39, 71

I-Thou, 64–65, 67, 71, 73, 75
imago Dei, 20, 22–25, 27–28,
    134
Irigaray, Luce, 157

Jefferson, Thomas, 3
Jesus
    absence of, 28, 82, 85, 90, 97
    ascension of, 84–86, 90,
        97–98
    as *autobasilea*, 20

death of, 21–22, 55, 70, 75
faithfulness of, 99, 164
presence of, 42, 75, 82,
    84–92, 95, 97–100
resurrection of, 21–22, 25,
    28, 84–85, 97–100
justification, doctrine of, 44–
    46, 108

Levinas, Emmanuel, 56, 64–68,
    70, 73
Lossky, Vladimir, 35
Luther, Martin, 87

McFadyen, Alistair, 92
Meyendorff, John, 41
Moore, G. E., 132–33

Nicea, Council of, 32, 39

occlusion, 17–18, 22, 37, 144

Paul, Saint
    on the body of Christ, 53–58,
        99, 101, 129–30
    and equality in Christ,
        109–12, 154
    on the eucharist, 91, 97
    and human nature, 137
    on justification, 108
    and love of neighbor, 76
poststructuralism, 16, 22, 24,
    126–28, 133

reciprocity, 12, 124–25
representation, 36–38, 42–45,
    60, 101
Rogers, Eugene F., 142, 145,
    155, 160

Book Notes

In the Company of Others:
A Dialogical Christology
David H. Jensen
Religion/Theology

David H. Jensen argues that Christians are primarily called to learn from people of other faiths rather than to convert them. He offers a discussion of the spectrum of Christian responses to the religious Other, from enemy to one whom we are summoned in love, and calls for a christological approach in dealing with others. He also discusses the potential that the concept of *kenosis* has for Christian-Buddhist dialogue as an example of how a self-emptying approach might promote interreligious conversation.

0-8298-1420-5, 224 pages, paper $16.00

Listening to the Least:
Doing Theology from the Outside In
Ian A. McFarland
Religion/Theology

Christians claim to teach with authority, but the church has supported serfdom, slavery, colonialism, anti-Semitism, the oppression of women, and other wrongs. Ian McFarland returns to the example of the ministry of Jesus. Like Jesus, he asserts, the church should build a community from the margins of society.

0-8298-1283-0, 166 pages, paper, $16.95

To order call 800-537-3394
Fax 216-736-2206
or visit our web site at
www.pilgrimpress.com

Prices do not include shipping and handling.
Prices subject to change without notice.